What is philosophy and what can it do for us? The long answer takes the rest of this book, but the short answer is that philosophy is a collection of problems and attempts to solve them. Does God exist? How should a human being try to live? Is it reasonable, or is it just inevitable, that we trust our senses? Is communication a transfer of ideas? What's the best way to improve our understanding of the world? These are the ground-level problems of philosophy and if none of them interest you, you should put this book down at once.

I take it you're still reading. Good. I said that those problems about God, morality, perception, meaning and science were the ground-level problems of philosophy, but there are others at ground level, and there are upper levels too. A ground-level question for political philosophy is 'Why should a citizen obey the government?' A ground-level question for aesthetics is 'What makes a thing beautiful?' But let's go up a level. Reflection on a ground-level problem quickly brings us up against some concepts we aren't very clear about. When we ask, for example, whether it's reasonable to trust our senses in the way we do, it soon becomes necessary to understand a bit more explicitly what we mean by the word 'reasonable'. What makes a belief a reasonable belief? What makes a person a reasonable person? This is something we would like to know even without the ground-level problem about perception, because the idea of reasonableness is obviously an important idea, and it would be good to gain a better understanding of it. In general, we can say that the second-level problems of philosophy involve the analysis or evolution of concepts, such as the concept of reason, or happiness, or existence, or knowledge, or causality.

However, at this point, we probably begin to feel a bit disoriented. We want a nice clear map, showing where the ground-level problems stand in relation to each other, where they ascend to second-level problems, how the second-level problems connect with each other. We want to know if there's a third level. We want sound advice about quick and reliable ways of getting around.

Well, the truth is, I can't offer you a map. At this stage in our history, there *is* no map. We're still finding our way around these wonderful, bewildering, problems. But don't despair. I can and do offer, in what follows, a *sketch* of a map. It's a bit rough, no doubt, and incomplete, but I think it helps.

Simply Philosophy

BRENDAN WILSON

Edinburgh University Press

© Brendan Wilson, 2002

Edinburgh University Press Ltd
22 George Square, Edinburgh

Typeset in Minion and Gill Sans
by Pioneer Associates, Perthshire, and
printed and bound in Great Britain by
Scotprint, Haddington, East Lothian

A CIP record for this book is available from the British Library

ISBN 0 7486 1568 7 (paperback)

The right of Brendan Wilson
to be identified as author of this work
has been asserted in accordance with
the Copyright, Designs and Patents Act 1988.

For Emma and Hugo

Contents

Area 6: Objectivity

Area 7: God

What is Philosophy?

Preface

This book is an introduction to philosophy – though unlike most introductions, it also has an argument. The argument is that the problems we try to solve in philosophy mostly derive from changes which have occurred in our idea of a cause, over the last two and a half millennia, from causes as purposes, to causes as impulses, to causes as correlations. The idea of causality also reveals connections between problems which seem at first sight quite unrelated, and so reveals the peculiarly *holistic* nature of philosophy: in philosophy, what we say about one problem has far-reaching consequences for what we are able to say about the others.

So causality does two things for us in this book – it explains how the central problems of philosophy arise, and it shows by example that they are not separate or separable from each other. Perhaps it's a bit ambitious to raise these large-scale issues in an introductory book. Yet one of the things any philosopher needs is a sense of the 'big picture', a rationale for the historical sequence and a map of the network of problems. The argument is that causality can provide all this.

The idea of a cause is obviously important in ordinary life – how many times a day do we say 'because'? But it has been made to work hardest in science, and so the nature of science is our first main concern. This is 'relevant' because we ourselves obviously live in an age of science, but it will also allow us to explore some of the problems involved in the idea of causality.

Our second question, beginning in Chapter 4, will be the reality of the mind. To say that something is real is, on one plausible account, to say that it has a causal role (connecting the problem of causality with metaphysics). So the question whether our thoughts are real becomes the question whether they can cause and be caused.

This leads to a problem about freedom: if our thoughts have to be part of the causal nexus in order to qualify as real, can they in that case be free? Chapters 7 and 8 show how the problem of causality connects with issues of action and responsibility. Chapters 9 and 10 explain the consequences for moral thinking.

The problem of causality also connects with epistemology (the group of problems concerning knowledge). Aristotle had explained genuine knowledge of a thing as knowledge of its *cause*, which he took to be (roughly speaking) its purpose, or reason for existing. When this teleological concept of a cause was jettisoned in the seventeenth century, a new account of knowledge was required. Chapters 11–15 deal with the development of this new account and its sceptical consequences.

The same new account of knowledge led, through its emphasis on introspection, to the view that our language abilities depend on interior mental processes. In Chapters 16–19, we look at three problems arising: classification, naming and communication.

The problem of causality and the infallibility of introspection are both involved in the problem of perception, which is the topic of Chapter 20. If an idea is caused by some external object, and if we cannot make mistakes about our own ideas, do we therefore have reliable information about their external causes?

The concept of a cause, whether we think of it as purpose (like Aristotle), as impulse (like Descartes), or as correlation (like Hume), also bears on the problem of truth. The principal purpose – hence 'cause' – of language is to convey truth, and a true statement is one correlated with – hence 'caused by' – reality. The problem of truth (discussed in Chapters 22–23) also follows on naturally from the problem of perception, since many if not all of the truths we know come to us through perception.

Truth in turn leads naturally to God, with whom we close. It is no accident that God has traditionally been understood not only as the source and knower of all truth, but also as both first *cause* and final *purpose* of the universe.

A diagram summarising the path we follow through the problems is given on page 205. There is much we only glimpse, and much we do not see at all, but perhaps an 'overview' will always sacrifice some of the detail for the sake of the bigger picture.

I am grateful to the following friends and colleagues, who read and commented on various drafts: J. Patrick Barron, Angus Collins, Clive Collins, Alex Dunbar, James G. Foulds, Ian Hargrave, Brian Harrison, Hidé Ishiguro, Sandra Lucore, Bill Newton-Smith, and Akiko Tsukamoto.

I am also indebted to my colleagues and students at the University of Tokyo for a very positive and friendly environment for teaching and research, and for making possible the period of sabbatical leave during which the book was completed.

How to read this book

On the left hand page you will find continuous text, which puts one person's view of the central problems of philosophy. The right hand page pretends to greater objectivity, giving relevant quotations (which I have tried to keep short and non-technical), illustrations, and occasionally, background information. At the end of each chapter there are three or four 'assertions'. These can be used to recall the main ideas of the chapter, or as launch-pads for further thought. If you are reading with others, you may find it interesting to try to reach consensus about them.

Simply Philosophy

CHAPTER 1

Progress

In this chapter, we consider two conflicting accounts of scientific progress. According to the common sense picture, scientists first collect data, and then devise a theory to explain it. This data-first model has been challenged by Karl Popper, who argues that scientists often devise a theory first, and only then go looking for data to test it.

We live in times of quite unprecedented progress. We have abilities – to extend life, generate energies, travel distances, investigate extremes – which were unimaginable only a hundred years ago. So we begin with the triumph of our age, with science, and in particular, with the *progress* of science. Whether by slow accumulation or dramatic restructuring, science seems to be able to build on previous results, and this gives it the air of making definite progress. Understanding how science advances, then, would be at least a large step towards understanding its success. And perhaps the answer to this question does not seem far to seek. Isn't it just common sense to say that, in science, we first collect data and then devise a theory to explain it?

This data-first model derives from the (rather more sophisticated) account of Francis Bacon (1561–1626), an English politician and scientist who lived when modern science was taking its first uncertain steps. In one of Bacon's metaphors, doing science is like making wine – first we gather in the grapes (data), then we press out the juice to make wine (theory).

Data-first or theory-first?

Recent times have seen a number of challenges to this traditional picture of science, some philosophical and some historical. Historically, it seems that a theory leads us, or enables us, to discover new data just as often as fresh data prompt us to devise a new theory. Then again, historical examples in which a theory appears to have been derived in classic Baconian fashion, are open to challenge. Newton presented his theory of universal gravitation as derived from Kepler's laws of planetary motion, along with observed phenomena such as tides, the famous apple and what-not. But in an influential critique, Pierre Duhem (1861–1916) argued that Newton's derivation was impossible. For one thing, Newton's theory involves new concepts (such as 'force' and 'mass') unknown to Kepler, and for another, it actually *conflicts* with Kepler's laws. Newton's theory predicts small deviations from the perfectly elliptical orbits predicted by Kepler.

DATA ⫸ THEORY

How science works (according to common sense)

God's mathematics

Since ancient times, it had been believed that because the circle is the perfect shape, and because the heavens must be perfect, planets must move in circles. If observations seem to show otherwise, then the planets must be moving in circles superimposed on other circles.

By the time of Copernicus (1473–1543), no fewer than seventy-seven of these superimposed circles were needed to account for the motions of the sun, moon and the five known planets. But if you expect to find God's mathematics in the universe – as both Copernicus and Kepler did – this seems scandalously complicated.

Copernicus managed to get the number of superimposed circles down to thirty-four, by placing the sun at the centre and assuming that the earth moves. But it was Kepler (1571–1630) who really revolutionised astronomy. His first law broke with tradition and 'logic' by supposing that the planets move, not in circles, but ellipses. The beautiful second law (also published in 1609) rejected the idea that the planets must move at constant speed, and explained how they speed up as they come closer to the sun and slow down as they move away from it. The third law (1619) stated the relationship between the time it takes for a planet to complete an orbit of the sun, and its average distance from the sun.

However, lack of a notion of gravity exposed Copernicus and Kepler to numerous embarrassing questions. What could move something as heavy as the earth? Why do we not fly off the earth like children off a merry-go-round? Why does the earth itself not fly to pieces? These and other objections were answered by Galileo and Newton.

Philosophically, there are two main problems with the common sense, data-first picture of science. First, it assumes that we can make observations before we have any theory (just as we can gather grapes before we have any wine). This assumption is, for several reasons, difficult to defend. For one thing, observation is always selective – we *choose* something from the welter of perception as the important thing – and choosing already seems to embody a primitive kind of theory. Then again, in order to say what we have seen, we have to use some form of language, which in its system of classifications, already contains an implicit theory of the world. Most of all, scientific observations would usually make no sense at all without a background of theory which allows us to interpret them. Auguste Comte (1798–1857) wrote: 'Since Bacon, all good intellects have agreed that there is no real knowledge save that which rests on observed facts . . . But if on the one hand every theory must be based on observation, on the other it is equally true that facts cannot be observed without the guidance of some theory.' And Comte's English contemporary, William Whewell (1794–1866), compressed the point into a powerful image when he said, '. . . there is a mask of theory over the whole face of nature . . .'.

The second philosophical problem is that it is not easy to explain in any explicit way how we get from data to theory. The process by which we arrive at a theory is as mysterious to us as fermentation once was to wine-makers. Some people (following Hume) have even concluded that the process is non-rational, that a theory cannot be rationally *justified* by reference to data.

One of these people, Sir Karl Popper (1902–1994), has put forward a new picture of science. He believes that since science *is* a rational activity, and since it cannot be rational if it begins with data, it must begin with theories. According to Popper, we first dream up a theory, then look around for data, trying to prove that the theory is *wrong*. If, after many attempts, we are unable to prove a theory wrong, we accept it (at least temporarily).

Which picture is correct? Or are both partly correct? Let's take an example . . .

The discovery of penicillin

Alexander Fleming (1881–1955) qualified as a doctor in 1906. When the First World War broke out, Fleming was working in the inoculation department of St. Mary's Hospital in London under Sir Almroth Wright. Wright, Fleming and other members of the department were sent to Boulogne to look after soldiers wounded in the war. In particular, they were asked to try to find the best way of treating infected wounds.

At that time, wounds were usually washed periodically with an antiseptic solution, which was known to kill bacteria outside the body. But Fleming

Francis Bacon

THEORY ⮕ DATA

How science works (according to Karl Popper)

quickly discovered that this method only seemed to help the bacteria. In fact, the antiseptic solution also killed the body's white blood cells, so that the patient's natural resistance to the bacteria was weakened. Wright and his group suggested that wounds should not be treated with antiseptics, but this counter-intuitive advice was ignored.

After the war, back in London, Fleming searched for something which would kill bacteria without killing white blood cells, and in 1921, he discovered an interesting substance called *lysozyme*. Fleming found lysozyme in saliva, in the eggs of birds and fish, in vegetables and flowers, and in the tears of more than fifty animals (including human animals). Lysozyme is able to kill about three-quarters of air-borne bacteria, and it does no harm to white blood cells. Unfortunately, it also does not kill any of the bacteria responsible for the most serious diseases.

A few years later, Fleming was working on the *Staphylococcus* group of bacteria. He was growing Staphylococci and simply leaving them at room temperature for a few days to see if they changed colour (the colour of a strain can help to show how dangerous it is). At first he was helped by D. M. Pryce, a research student, but Pryce left to take another job in February 1928. Fleming worked on by himself until August, when he went for his usual summer holiday. Early in September, Pryce called in to see Fleming, and found him in the middle of post-holiday tidying up. The petri dishes containing the Staphylococci had been left out on the laboratory bench all through August, and now Fleming was cleaning them, ready for more experiments. Fleming began to complain about having too much to do, and at random, picked up a petri dish to show Pryce. According to Pryce, Fleming then stopped suddenly, stared at the petri dish for a while and said: 'That's funny'. This was the dish containing penicillin.

Fleming showed the dish to his colleagues in the laboratory, but none of them thought it was very interesting. Fleming, however, saw that some kind of mould was killing the Staphylococci. At first, he thought this mould was *Penicillium rubrum*, but in fact it was *Penicillium notatum*, a much rarer kind. He inferred that the mould was producing a substance which killed the bacteria colonies in the dish.

Fleming produced more of the mould, and filtered it to give what he called 'mould juice'. His tests showed that this 'mould juice' was able to kill the bacteria responsible for several serious diseases. And miraculously, it did not harm white blood cells at all.

The discovery of penicillin owed a great deal to luck. *Penicillium notatum* will only grow in cool conditions and sure enough, the beginning of August 1928 was unusually cool in London. Also, *Penicillium notatum* is very rare, and probably came by accident from a nearby laboratory which was investigating

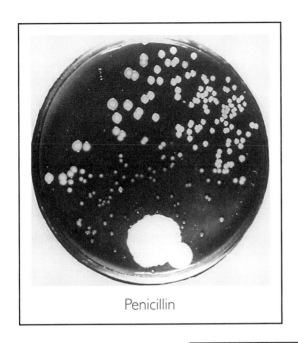

Penicillin

Alexander Fleming

connections between moulds and asthma. Other kinds of *Penicillium* produce very little penicillin. But now Fleming's luck gave out. Penicillin was difficult to keep in good condition, and tests gave mixed results. He gradually came to believe that penicillin could not kill bacteria inside the body. It was useful in laboratory work, and Fleming continued to make it, and to send samples to other labs. But he lost faith in it as an effective medicine. It was not until 1941, in the middle of another World War, that penicillin was established as a 'wonder drug'.

Conclusion

Which picture of science does this important discovery support? Fleming saw that the Staphylococci in the dish he showed Pryce were dying. He then suggested, as an explanation, that the mould was producing a substance which killed bacteria. Data first, then theory, as Bacon says. But the data (a small dish with spots on it) only made sense to him because of a great deal of theory. Theory first, then data. Also, Fleming went on to test his explanation thoroughly, using various bacteria and white blood cells. Theory first, then tests, as Popper says. As a result of the data from these tests, Fleming came to believe that penicillin could not work effectively in the body and gave up that line of research. Data first, then theory.

It's easy to say that science makes progress by a kind of 'leveraged ascent' – a bit of data, then a bit of theory, then a bit more data, then a bit more theory, and so on. But that doesn't answer the questions which really separate the two pictures. Which comes first, data or theory? And how do we move, in any rational way, from data to theory?

We tend to be rather dismissive about 'luck'. To say that someone was lucky is, in ordinary speech, to deny them any credit. But as we also say – 'Fortune favours a prepared mind'.

...DATA ⇒ THEORY ⇒ DATA ...

Which comes first? And what do those arrows represent?

Do you agree ...?

1. **We can collect data unprejudiced by any theory.**

   _____

2. **Creating theories is a rational process.**

   _____

3. **Fleming's colleagues didn't understand the significance of the petri dish because they were stupid.**

   _____

4. **We cannot devise a theory without data.**

   _____

CHAPTER 2

Causes

This chapter introduces two problems about causality: first, what exactly does it mean to say that A caused B? and second, how reasonable is it to depend on our beliefs about causes?

We ended Chapter 1 with two questions. Let's consider the second one first. Is there a rational way to get from data to theory?

First, we need a clearer idea of what we mean by 'data' or 'observations' on one hand, and 'theory' or 'explanation' on the other. Relative to Tycho Brahe's observations, Kepler's laws of planetary motion were theory or explanation. But relative to Newton's theory of gravity, these same laws were data.

So let's suppose that the words 'data' and 'theory' are normally used in tandem. Given a particular data/theory pair, the 'data' will tend to be linked more closely to sensory input, and will tend to serve as the basis which justifies or leads to the 'theory'. Our interest in this chapter is that 'justifies or leads to'.

David Hume (1711–1776) was perhaps the greatest figure of the Scottish Enlightenment. Adam Smith (admittedly a friend of his) said that he 'approached as nearly to the idea of a perfectly wise and virtuous man, as perhaps the nature of human frailty will admit'. In his *Treatise of Human Nature* (1739), Hume pointed out something troubling about the concept of a cause and about causal reasoning.

The concept of a cause

When we say 'A caused B' we normally mean 'A made B happen'. We imagine that A compelled B to happen, or brought B about in such a way that B *had* to happen. But Hume points out that, strictly speaking, we never *observe* this 'compulsion'. All we really observe is A followed by B, then, sometime later, something resembling A followed by something resembling B, then, sometime later again, something else resembling A followed by something else resembling B – and so on. We never see A *making* B happen. All we see is A (and other A-like things) followed by B (and other B-like things).

Let's take an example. Suppose you are playing billiards. You hit the cue ball, which rolls across the table and collides with the object ball, which then begins to move. At the same moment, an onlooker coughs. What we observe on this occasion, taken strictly by itself, is only the cue ball moving from X to Y, two sounds (a click and a cough), and the object ball moving from Y to Z.

David Hume

Hume had a rather varied and interesting life. Law student, apprentice merchant, tutor to a deranged nobleman, soldier, librarian, diplomat – the thing he wanted most in life was to become famous as a writer, and this he abundantly achieved, becoming by his fifties adored in Paris, notorious in Scotland, and disparaged by 'the barbarians who live on the banks of the Thames'. He was probably the first writer to become wealthy through book receipts (as opposed to patronage).

As a person, he seems to have been cheerful and gregarious.

Hume on (not) perceiving causes:

'All events seem entirely loose and separate. One event follows another; but we never can observe any tie between them. They seem *conjoined*, but never *connected*. And as we can have no idea of anything which never appeared to our outward sense or inward sentiment, the necessary conclusion seems to be that we have no idea of connection or power at all, and that these words are absolutely without any meaning . . .' *Enquiry* (1748)

Notice the movement of thought here: **no experience** (of connection or power) . . . **therefore no idea** (of connection or power) . . . **therefore no meaning** (in the words 'connection' or 'power').

This is radical empiricism in action, and we will see the same line of thought applied to other topics before long.

All these events seem quite distinct – as Hume says 'loose and separate' – from each other. We don't observe any special tie or connection between any of them. How do we know, then, that the movement of the cue ball, and not the onlooker's cough, caused the object ball to begin to move? *Only* (Hume says) because we know that previous impacts have, and previous coughs have not, been correlated with movement.

Now Hume, as a good empiricist, wants to show how all our concepts derive from our sensory experience. How could our ordinary concept of a cause contain an element (of 'compulsion' or '*making* happen') which we never experience? It seems that, without any basis in experience, this element must be without any clear meaning. The remainder of the concept, which *is* based in experience, and which *is* therefore clear and justifiable, sees a cause as only a matter of constant conjunction (between A-like things and B-like things). This is disturbing because it means that our ordinary concept of a cause, to which we are naturally attached, is defective and has to be changed. If Hume is right, we have to stop saying that A *made* B happen.

Is it true to say that causality is only intelligible as constant conjunction? A common sense objection was raised by Hume's contemporary, Thomas Reid (1710–1796). Reid pointed out that day is constantly conjoined with night and night with day, though it would obviously be wrong to say that day causes night, or vice versa. You might suppose that Hume could meet this point rather easily, by saying that the constant conjunction of day and night reveals a causal relationship between both of them and something else (the rotation of the earth). They are constantly conjoined because they are both effects of some other cause. But then why is the rotation-day correlation causal, if the day-night correlation is not? Hume seems to need some further, not-yet-revealed criterion in order to distinguish causal correlations from non-causal ones. And if he is right to say that only constant conjunction is given in experience, it follows that this new criterion, whatever it might be, will be something not given in experience, and so unavailable, at least to Hume. Should he bite the bullet, then, and say that – surprising as it seems – a given day *does* cause the following night, which in turn *does* cause the succeeding day? Is that how radical an empiricist has to be about causes and effects?

Causal reasoning

So much for the problem of what it means to say 'A caused B'. The story so far is that it cannot mean that A made B happen, but only that A-like things are constantly conjoined with B-like things. Let's turn now to causal reasoning. When I wake up, see that the roads are wet and think 'It must have rained during the night', I arrive at a belief by reasoning from an observation (the wet

David Hume

Hume on our idea of a cause:

'We have no other notion of cause and effect, but that of certain objects, which have been *always conjoin'd* together, and which in all past instances have been found inseparable.' *Treatise* (1739)

Another example of radical empiricism, from Thomas Hobbes (1588–1678):

'. . . the knowledge of what is infinite can never be attained by a finite inquirer. Whatsoever we know that are men, we learn it from our phantasms [ideas]; and of infinite, whether magnitude or time, there is no phantasm at all; so that it is impossible for a man or any other creature to have a conception of infinite.' *De Corpore* (1656)

roads) and a causal regularity (rain makes the roads wet). In the same way, when I see storm clouds gathering and think 'It's going to rain', I arrive at a belief (this time about the future) by reasoning from another observation and another causal regularity.

Hume pointed out that causal inferences like these are not deductive. When we think, 'The sun has risen millions of times in the past, so it will rise tomorrow too', this is a form of reasoning deeply unlike 'The sun has risen millions of times in the past, so it has risen more than a thousand times in the past'. The second of these is deductive: if the premisses are true, the conclusion *must* be true. But the premiss(es) of the first, causal, kind of reasoning could be true and in spite of that, the conclusion could be false. The sun might not rise tomorrow, in spite of its exemplary past record. As Russell said, the chicken which reasons, 'That nice farmer has always fed me in the past, so he will feed me again today' may be in for a nasty shock, if today happens to be Christmas.

But if the conclusion of a causal inference could be false, what justifies us in believing it? Why should we believe something that could be false? If there was some kind of compulsion linking cause to effect, perhaps that could justify us in believing that the effect will occur, given the cause. But Hume has already ruled that out.

Then perhaps we can add an extra premiss to the argument, to make it deductive after all. For example, we might argue 'The sun has risen millions of times in the past, and the future will resemble the past, so the sun will rise tomorrow too.' This argument is deductively valid: if the premisses are true, the conclusion must be true. But is the premiss we have added true? Why should we believe that the future will always resemble the past (or that nature obeys unchanging laws, or any other 'principle of induction')?

Hume argues that we could try to show that the added premiss is true either on the basis of experience, or independently of experience. If independently of experience, then we would be proving something informative *about* the world (that the world behaves in a certain regular way) independently of all experience *of* the world. Well, where would this information come from? For an empiricist, information about the world (for example, that the future will resemble the past) comes only from experience.

So we would have to try to justify the premiss we added, from experience. Perhaps we could argue like this . . .

1. The future relative to 1900 resembled the past relative to 1900.
2. The future relative to 1901 resembled the past relative to 1901.
3. Etc. etc. etc.
N. Therefore, the future relative to this year will resemble the past relative to this year.

Hume on the impossibility of justifying induction:

'All probable arguments are built on the supposition, that there is this conformity betwixt the future and the past, and therefore can never prove it. This conformity is a *matter of fact*, and if it must be proved, will admit of no proof but from experience. But our experience in the past can be a proof of nothing for the future, but upon a supposition, that there is a resemblance betwixt them. This therefore is a point, which can admit of no proof at all, and which we take for granted without any proof.' *Treatise* (1739)

Popper's (radical) reaction to Hume:

'Hume, I felt, was perfectly right in pointing out that induction cannot be logically justified. He held that there can be no valid logical arguments allowing us to establish "*that those instances, of which we have had no experience, resemble those, of which we have had experience*". Consequently "*even after the observation of the frequent or constant conjunction of objects, we have no reason to draw any inference concerning any object beyond those of which we have had experience . . .*". As a result we can say that theories can never be inferred from observation statements, or rationally justified by them . . . I found Hume's refutation of inductive inference clear and conclusive.' *Conjectures and Refutations* (1963)

Unfortunately, *this* argument is not deductively valid. Even though the premisses are all true, the conclusion could be false. And so this supporting argument also needs an extra premiss, which in turn needs to be justified either from experience or independently of experience, and round about the mulberry bush we go.

One response to all this is to accept it as a refutation of causal reasoning. A less radical response is to say that a conclusion is not unreasonable just because it *could* be false. If the chance of it being false is very small, it's surely reasonable to believe it. So can't we justify our belief that the sun will rise tomorrow by saying that the chance of it being false is very small? Yes we can. But it will now be asked how we know that the chance of the conclusion being false is very small. What justifies *this* claim? The answer, of course, is that the sun has risen lots of times in the past, which takes us straight back to square one. If we don't arrive at our belief that the sun will rise deductively (accepting that Hume was right about this), how *do* we arrive at it?

Induction

The easy answer is that we get there *in*ductively. But this is easy because it gives us just a name. What *is* inductive reasoning? When, exactly, is an inductive inference justified, and to what degree? Most of us are reasonably good at weighing probabilities in an intuitive way, and great scientists (or great gamblers) are unusually intuitive in this sense. They are good at guessing right. But we do not yet – we really do not – have any agreed account of how these guesses at probability work. As a matter of fact, we do not even have an agreed account of what it *means* to say that something is probable.

Hume, however, had a very clear account of our natural faculty of guesswork. He compares the human imagination to a galley, put into motion by the oars and continuing under its own momentum when the oars are raised. Past experiences of A+B propel the imagination, confronted in the present with something resembling A, to imagine B. And vividly imagining B, on Hume's analysis of belief, is not to be distinguished from believing that B will occur. Our belief that B will occur is therefore a product of the natural inertia of the imagination, or in more modern terms, it is a kind of conditioned reflex. Highly sophisticated no doubt, but not *reasoned*. Our belief that the sun will rise tomorrow is a psychological reaction we cannot help, not a judgment we can rationally justify. In the same way, *all* our expectations about the future, all our causal inferences about the unobserved present or past, if Hume is right, are just unreasoned products of psychological conditioning.

As Quine (1908–2000) said, 'Induction itself is essentially only . . . animal expectation or habit formation'. Pavlov, considered as a causal reasoner, is no more rational than his salivating dog.

Probability

When someone says a coin has a 50 per cent chance of landing heads up, does that mean:

A. that if this coin was tossed a million times, it would land heads up 500,000 times, or

B. that for the single throw in question, the speaker feels no more confident about a head turning up than a tail, or

C. that our evidence, prior to tossing the coin, leaves open two possibilities (heads or tails) and since landing heads is one out of these two, the claim that it will land heads has a one in two chance of being true.

Battles continue to rage between adherents of these Frequentist, Subjectivist and Range theories of probability, and there are pretty serious problems with all three. Our ordinary notion of probability resists analysis – so far.

Do you agree . . . ?

1. **It is reasonable to believe that the sun will rise tomorrow.**

2. **We never observe one thing making another happen.**

3. **We constantly assume, without proof, that the future will resemble the past.**

4. **To say that A caused B is not just to say that A's are correlated with B's.**

CHAPTER 3

Probability

In this chapter, we look in more detail at Popper's theory-first picture of scientific progress. I argue, against Popper, that the data-first picture is closer to the truth, and that data *can* justify a theory, though we don't yet understand very clearly how that kind of justification works.

We don't seem to have made much progress. Well, the fact is that we *don't* know in any explicit way how data justifies or leads to theory. So here, by contrast, is an answer to the other question with which we ended Chapter 1: which comes first, data or theory? In any particular data/theory pair, most of the data come first, most of the time.

This does not mean that there must be some absolutely primitive data, underlying all the rest, because the term 'theory' starts to lose application as we move towards more and more primitive data (and when one term in the pair goes, so does the other). Are we going to call 'The litmus paper turned red' a *theory*? If not, we needn't look for 'data' (such as raw input from the senses) to support it.

From data to theory

However, we *are* saying that data can lead to theory, somehow or other. Popper, convinced by Hume's brilliant and disturbing analysis, claims that data can rationally show a theory to be false, but cannot rationally show it to be true, or even probable. It follows that if causal reasoning is a rational procedure – as we would all like to think – it must operate by devising theories and trying to show them to be false. The basic method of science, according to Popper, is not verification, but falsification.

Still, even Popper allows us to believe, however tentatively, a theory which has survived numerous attempts to falsify it. So let's compare a theory which has survived a hundred attacks, with a new theory which, so far, has survived only half a dozen (supposing the attacks to be of equal vigour). Can't we repose more confidence in the hundred-survivor than the half-a-dozen-survivor? If no, then why is there a difference between surviving one attack and remaining untested? But if yes, then we have degrees of justification, and so at least an analogue of degrees of probability after all. We can concede to Popper that data (from the tests devised to attack the theory) may indeed follow our first conjecture of the theory, and that they may sometimes serve to falsify rather than support the theory. But we retain the common sense claims

Karl Popper

DATA ➠ CONJECTURE ➠ data ➠ ACCEPTANCE

(Lower case 'data' for test results)

that data normally precede in time, and can also serve to justify, our acceptance of the theory.

A (small) victory for common sense. But now we have to face Popper's claim that data cannot *support* a theory, but only omit to show it to be false. Is this true?

Suppose I am shown the three-card trick, and asked which card is the queen. I say the middle card. I am invited to turn the card over, and behold, it *is* the queen. This surely does more than merely omit to demolish my 'theory': it establishes that I was right. Would anyone in his or her right mind go on to check that the cards to the right and left are *not* the queen? And would they feel *more* confident that the middle card really is the queen if, on turning the right and left cards over, they were seen not to be the queen? Turning over the middle card provides 'data' which conclusively verify my 'theory' that the middle card is the queen.

It may be objected that this is a bad analogy. A real scientific theory, of course, does not consist of a single prediction, and the success of a single prediction does not establish it. But then my 'theory' that the middle card is the queen does not lead to only one prediction either. It also predicts that the left-hand card is not the queen. I might make *that* prediction first and test it. I look and sure enough, the left-hand card is not the queen. This observation does not establish my theory, but neither does it demolish it.

Two ways to support a theory

There seem then to be two sorts of test, establishing and non-demolishing. If we think real scientific theories are *very* unlike the three-card trick analogy – in issuing no make-or-break predictions of the 'queen in the middle' type – then we will think all scientific tests are of the non-demolishing kind. And if we think real scientific theories are *very* unlike the three-card trick – in having an indefinitely large number of possible tests – then we will think that surviving a test will in practice add nothing to the theory's probability. To rule out one option from three (by turning over the left-hand card) seems to improve the theory's chance of being true from one in three to one in two. But to rule out one option from indefinitely many is no significant improvement.

In fact, it's hard to believe that no scientific tests at all are of the establishing kind. Einstein's General Theory of Relativity predicted, among many other things, certain astronomical observations. Light from distant stars should be deflected by the sun, and so should be visible to us during an eclipse. On Newtonian principles, the distant stars should be hidden behind the sun. In 1919, three years after the theory was published, the necessary eclipse occurred, and the distant stars were indeed observed (by teams sent to

The bending of starlight

.

(In this diagram, the dot represents the earth. The sun wouldn't fit — you have to imagine it. It's about the size of a pea, and it's at arm's length from the dot. The distant stars whose light was deflected by the sun's gravity — less than two sixtieths of a sixtieth of a degree — are a good five thousand miles away on the same scale.)

Brazil and West Africa). This seems much more like the 'queen in the middle' kind of prediction, than the 'queen not on the left' kind. The result of the test seems to do more than merely omit to demolish the theory. It does not *establish* the theory, because the theory involves much more than this, but it does seem to support it in some positive, and indeed dramatic, way.

Here's a 'cleaner' example. The periodic table of elements was devised by the Russian chemist Dmitri Mendeleyev in 1869. Mendeleyev (1834–1907) simply wanted to put the information then known about the elements into some systematic form. His dependence on this information was so complete that it's debatable whether the table should be called a theory at all (rather than a taxonomy), but since it gives rise to predictions, let's not quibble. The table organises the elements in order of increasing atomic weight, but also places those with similar chemical properties in the same columns. Light, unstable metals form a column. Elements which combine with oxygen in the ratio two atoms to three form another, and so on. However, at that time, when only sixty-three elements were known, there were some holes where elements 'ought' to have been. No known elements existed to occupy the spaces below aluminium, silicon or boron, for example.

Such was Mendeleyev's confidence in his table that he publicly predicted the existence of these elements, specifying their approximate atomic weights and making rather detailed predictions about their chemical properties. Respectable chemists scoffed. And then people started *finding* his elements. The discovery of gallium in 1875, scandium soon after, and germanium in 1886, each possessing the various properties Mendeleyev had predicted for them, seemed to do much more than merely omit to demolish Mendeleyev's predictions. They seemed to establish pretty conclusively that he was right.

How science progresses

If, as these examples seem to show, theories can be positively supported, rather than merely not demolished, then Popper's account is leaving something important out. But here's a complication. I said that Mendeleyev's dependence on the existing data about the elements was complete, and so it was. Unfortunately, the data wouldn't all fit. The atomic weight of gold, and the atomic weight of tellurium, put them both into the 'wrong' columns. Once again, Mendeleyev's confidence in the *structure* he had seen in the rest of the data led him to assert (without empirical tests) that the accepted values for these atomic weights were just wrong. The true atomic weight of tellurium, he insisted, would be found to be less than that of iodine. The true atomic weight of gold would be found to be greater than that of platinum. Further tests proved him right about this too. Here we see theory generating

Dmitri Mendeleyev

1																	2
H																	He
3	4											5	6	7	8	9	10
Li	Be											B	C	N	O	F	Ne
11	12											13	14	15	16	17	18
Na	Mg											Al	Si	P	S	Cl	Ar
19	20	21	22	23	24	25	26	27	28	29	30	31	32	33	34	35	36
K	Ca	Sc	Ti	V	Cr	Mn	Fe	Co	Ni	Cu	Zn	Ga	Ge	As	Se	Br	Kr
37	38	39	40	41	42	43	44	45	46	47	48	49	50	51	52	53	54
Rb	Sr	Y	Zr	Nb	Mo	Tc	Ru	Rh	Pd	Ag	Cd	In	Sn	Sb	Te	I	Xe
55	56	57	72	73	74	75	76	77	78	79	80	81	82	83	84	85	86
Cs	Ba	La	Hf	Ta	W	Re	Os	Ir	Pt	Au	Hg	Tl	Pb	Bi	Po	At	Rn
87	88	89	104	105	106	107	108	109	110	111	112		114		116		118
Fr	Ra	Ac	Rf	Db	Sg	Bh	Hs	Mt									

58	59	60	61	62	63	64	65	66	67	68	69	70	71
Ce	Pr	Nd	Pm	Sm	Eu	Gd	Tb	Dy	Ho	Er	Tm	Yb	Lu
90	91	92	93	94	95	96	97	98	99	100	101	102	103
Th	Pa	U	Np	Pu	Am	Cm	Bk	Cf	Es	Fm	Md	No	Lr

The modern periodic table of elements

predictions and a programme of tests (so that we have lots of data, then a theory, then some more data to confirm it). But more interestingly, we also see a theory overriding some of the data on which it is based. So although (most of) the data comes first, as I said above, some of that data can be re-evaluated and some of it even rejected, at least provisionally, for the sake of an otherwise convincing theory. It's also worth noticing that the (perhaps smaller) amount of data which comes *after* the theory has particular importance, as Bacon said, because it's harder to get a prediction right than just to offer an explanation after the event.

One last, extra, complication: Mendeleyev's table was theory, relative to the existing data about atomic weights and chemical characteristics. But the table was also crucial evidence in the effort to understand atomic structure. Relative to Bohr's 1913 theory of the structure of the atom, Mendeleyev's table (now containing various new elements and a whole new column) was data. But this confirms what we said above about data/theory pairs.

Like most people, then, and unlike Hume and Popper, I think some causal beliefs are more probable than others. I suppose it *is* more reasonable, because more probable, to believe that the sun will rise tomorrow. I just can't explain *how it is* that past sunrises legitimise the expectation of future ones. Still, we're working on that. And I suppose that to realise we need to work on it is progress of a sort – progress which we owe to Hume.

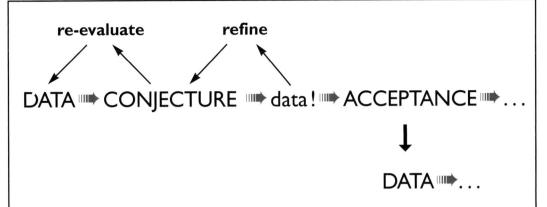

re-evaluate   refine

DATA ➠ CONJECTURE ➠ data! ➠ ACCEPTANCE ➠ . . .

↓

DATA ➠ . . .

Some of the main stages in scientific progress (where the horizontal arrows indicate some not-yet-explicitly-understood process of inductive reasoning, and the vertical arrow represents the decision to treat an accepted theory as data).

Do you agree . . . ?

1. Mendeleyev's theory was a lucky guess, not a rational inference.

    _____

2. The three-card trick is not a fair analogy for a scientific theory.

    _____

3. Scientific theories are accepted because their rivals fail, not because they themselves are well-supported.

    _____

4. Even 'Cats have whiskers', strictly speaking, is a theory.

    _____

CHAPTER 4

A Real Idea

In this chapter, we establish a connection between causality and real existence: to say that something really exists (on one natural interpretation) is to say that it can cause and be caused. This means that if we don't clearly understand causality, as Chapters 1–3 suggested, we don't clearly understand what it means to say that something is real.

So far we have been looking at some of the difficulties surrounding the notion of a cause, and showing how they bear on our attempts to understand how science makes progress. In the present chapter we relate the concept of a cause to the concept of reality, and in particular, to the reality of thought.

Let's begin with a little thought-experiment. Start saying the alphabet to yourself, in your head. Let ten or twenty seconds pass. Stop. Now suppose you drop dead. None of those you leave behind you knows what the last letter you said to yourself was. Nobody in the world knows. And yet there *was* a 'last letter you said to yourself'. If only you had survived, you could have told us what it was.

What's interesting about this? Well, there was something real to you, something which you knew about and could have revealed to us, but which was, as it were, quite unreal to everybody else. As far as the rest of us were concerned, nothing was going on. And this notion of 'real-only-to-N' is odd. We want to say that if something's real, it's *real*, and that's that. What's even odder is that we all seem to know about quite a large category of events and 'objects', which are 'real-to-me' and at any rate far-from-obvious to everybody else.

These questions of mental reality were important to Descartes (1596–1650), a French scientist, mathematician and philosopher who died of giving philosophy tutorials, at five o'clock in the morning, to the Queen of Sweden. (Unused to the cold Swedish mornings, he caught pneumonia.) We'll look at Descartes' influential views on the reality of the mind in a moment, but our first step (just as it was with the terms 'data' and 'theory') is to get a bit clearer about the meaning of the word 'real'. When we say something's *real*, what do we mean?

A real Chippendale

If we say a Chippendale is real, we mean it was made by Thomas of that ilk in the eighteenth century. If we say a tarantula is real, we mean it isn't a plastic

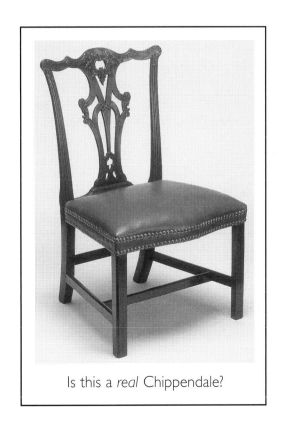

Is this a *real* Chippendale?

imitation. 'Real' in this kind of usage means 'not a copy or simulacrum'. And *that* means, usually, that the thing in question has the origins, or the properties, of something else which is held up as the standard. 'She's a real lady' emphasises properties (she behaves in a civilised and courteous way): 'He's a real Duke' emphasises origins (he comes from an aristocratic family). I suppose this 'origins and properties' sense underlies the cases where we say something's real, meaning that it's among the best of its type. 'Now that's what I call a real painting' might contrast, say, a representational with an abstract painting and express a preference for the former. The speaker likes the painting in question because it has a certain origin, or more probably in this case, certain properties.

The 'origins and properties' sense also underlies cases like 'He was a real coward'. This might not mean that he acted like a coward (had the properties of a coward) on one particular occasion. It might mean that his cowardice was a settled and reliable trait of character. In this case, 'real' means exemplary or stereotypical, or something like that. But that too is a kind of property – he had the expected properties of a coward (running away from danger, imagining threats where none exist etc.) and in addition, the property of doing this in a settled and reliable way. This additional property makes the speaker's disapproval all the stronger.

Perhaps the 'origins and properties' sense also underlies cases where we talk about emotions as real. When we say, 'It was real love', we mean (usually) that the emotion was genuine, not produced by peer-suggestion, or self-deception. And in addition, that it was strong and enduring. In short, it had a certain origin ('It came from the heart') and certain properties.

A real dagger

Unfortunately, there's another meaning of 'real' (or another family of them). The dagger seen by Macbeth wasn't real, it was a figment of his imagination, or an illusion produced by the witches. Then of course, there *was* a real Macbeth (in the eleventh century), whereas Hamlet is fictional. In this sense, 'real' does not mean 'not a copy'. It means – not a dream, not a myth, not fictional, not imaginary, and so on. In this second sense, a plastic tarantula or fake Chippendale is perfectly real.

Can't we say anything more positive about this second meaning? Not-this, not-that, not-the-other seems a bit feeble. After all, this is the sense of 'real' we're particularly interested in when we ask about the reality of thoughts. We don't want to know if your mental recitation of the alphabet was a copy of a real alphabet, or whether it was exemplary. We want to know if it *really* happened (in spite of its having been undetectable to all the rest of us).

'Is this a dagger that I see before me?'

Origins and properties seemed to underlie the 'not a copy' sense, so perhaps they can help here too. Not any particular origin (like the factory of Thomas Chippendale) or particular properties (like civilised behaviour), but the mere fact of *having* an origin and properties. Macbeth's dagger had an origin and properties too, however, so we need to be more specific. And perhaps our best idea (since Plato changed his mind about it in a late dialogue called the *Sophist*) is that *causal* origin and *causal* properties are crucial. That is, if something can be causally influenced by other things, and can causally affect them in its turn, then it's real. To be real, in our second sense, is to have a causal role.

A causal role

Does that seem like progress? Not much, because it all depends what 'causal' means. Aristotle (384–322BC) had a typically well-thought-out account of this. According to Aristotle, most things have a natural tendency towards a particular end-state, and when we grasp what this end-state is, we then understand whatever-it-is in the best possible way.

Let's take an example. Suppose a sculptor casts a bronze statue for a public festival in honour of some general or poet. Aristotle says there are four different kinds of cause we might investigate in a situation like this:
1. the *material* cause of the statue explains the material from which it was made, in this case bronze,
2. the *formal* cause explains why the statue has the form it has, referring perhaps to the mould in which it was cast,
3. the *efficient* cause tells us what happened to bring the statue into existence, the efficient cause of the statue being, let's say, the decision of the sculptor to create it,
4. the *final* cause explains the purpose or *raison d'être* of the statue – that for the sake of which it exists. It is *because* the statue is to be displayed at the festival that the sculptor decided to make it of such-and-such material and in such-and-such a form.

Aristotle, perhaps influenced by his work in biology, believed that final causes are the most important for scientific understanding. In the above example, the final cause is 'final' partly because it refers to the statue's end-state (standing on display), and partly because it explains all the other kinds of cause and so ends the process of explanation. The statue's final cause is 'that for the sake of which' all the other causes are the way they are.

Descartes, however, attacked the idea of natural purpose which was central to this Aristotelian concept of causality, and brought in a more mechanistic concept, based on the transmission of impulse. Rejecting Aristotle's

Plato (427–347BC), speaking through the Eleatic Stranger, on reality:

'I suggest that whatever has any natural capacity either to make something else different or to be affected even to the smallest extent by the slightest cause, even if only once, everything like this really exists. This power is the distinguishing mark of things that are real.'

Some examples of final causes:

Why do plants have leaves? To provide shade for the fruit. (Well, in this case, Aristotle got it wrong, but *our* answer – to catch sunlight for photosynthesis – takes the same, teleological, form.)

Why do animals have eyes? So that they can see. Again, the answer is in terms of the *purpose* of the eye, and this time – of course – we agree.

Why do for example cows have *brown* eyes? This, for Aristotle, is just a brute fact. Eye colour has no purpose, no final cause.

teleological concept of a 'final cause', Descartes wrote: '. . . the species of cause termed final finds no useful employment in physical things'.

This was a leap in the dark for our understanding of the mind, because whereas thoughts, mental images, decisions, mental rehearsals and so on often have a purpose (and so qualify as causal under the old Aristotelian concept), it's much more problematic whether they can receive and transmit anything like impulses. But if it's harder to see how thoughts could have a causal role (now that causes are to be understood in terms of mechanical impulse), and if having a causal role is what makes things real, then it's suddenly hard to believe that thoughts are real.

Here's Locke being brisk about mental impacts:

'The next thing to be considered, is how *bodies* produce *ideas* in us, and that is manifestly *by impulse*, the only way which we can conceive bodies operate in.' *Essay* (1689)

Do you agree . . . ?

1. **Saying the letter 'H' to yourself is a real mental event.**

   _____

2. **Something's real if you can touch it.**

   _____

3. **Time is unreal.**

   _____

4. **It's a mistake to equate reality with causal efficacy.**

   _____

CHAPTER 5

Body and Mind

This chapter continues to investigate the connection between causality and real existence, taking the reality of our thoughts as a test case. We see how the change from causes-as-purposes to causes-as-impulses led Descartes to a new, and deeply problematic, view of the reality of the mind.

Our problem, at the moment, is this: if we abandon final causes in favour of mechanical impulses, it seems that decisions, memories, ideas and all the other items in our mental lives must operate by impulse too, if they operate at all. That seems a bit odd, though we might note in passing that if Hume's analysis of causality is correct (Chapter 2) then there's no problem at all about a causal role for mental events. As long as there's a correlation between a given kind of mental event and a given kind of physical event, then according to Hume, there's causality. However, as we said before, Hume's analysis of causality is really rather shocking.

Descartes' equation

So Descartes has to relate the mental to the great vortex of particle collisions which make up physical reality. Where do thoughts fit into the bump and grind of material interaction? As if this wasn't difficult enough, there's a complication. Descartes also believes that our knowledge of the mental is far more secure, far more certain than any knowledge we have of external things. If you tell me that the last letter you said to yourself in your mental rehearsal of the alphabet was 'H', that seems to be a thing beyond all doubt for you. And I am certainly not in any position to contradict you. In short, if you know anything at all, you know what's happening in your own (conscious) mental life.

Knowledge of the external world, by contrast, is rather insecure, according to Descartes. Everything we seem to know about external things could conceivably be wrong. All that stuff we think we know – about ships and sealing wax, cabbages and kings – *could* all be a dream, Descartes says. Or there *could* be an evil demon, arranging illusions to deceive me. In a more modern form of the fantasy, my brain could have been removed into a vat, where the appropriate nerves are supplied with just the stimuli they would get if I really were seated in front of my computer etc. etc. (In Chapter 11, we'll look again at this Cartesian doubt.)

René Descartes

MIND/BODY
CAUSALITY

+

CERTAINTY
OF
INTROSPECTION

+

REALITY AS
THE BASIS OF
KNOWLEDGE

+

DEGREES OF
REALITY

= ?

Now if, as Descartes believes, our knowledge of things mental is the foundation of our knowledge of the external world, this makes it difficult to regard the mental as in any way second-class. In particular, it makes it difficult to regard the mental as less real than, or as depending for its reality on, the physical. (Here you see the influence of another concept of reality – as whatever is the ultimate source of our knowledge.)

To complicate matters even further, Descartes adopted from his predecessors the idea that our thoughts themselves have differing degrees of reality. I have an idea of a unicorn, of a tree in my garden, of God, and these (it seemed to Descartes and his predecessors) are importantly different. My idea of a unicorn is an artefact, a human creation. It corresponds to nothing in the real world. My idea of the tree is more real than this, because I didn't make the idea, and I don't have any choice about experiencing it. If I happen to look in the right direction – pop! – there it is. I *could* have created my idea of the tree (it was within my power to do so) but in fact it derives from something real. My idea of God, on the other hand, is something beyond all human powers of creation (because it is an idea of something infinitely powerful and good). Neither does it come to me from experience (for the same reason). Descartes concludes that it must come to me from God himself, and as Descartes believes that God is supremely real, the idea of God, too, is more real than any other.

According to Descartes, then, ideas are either factitious (made by us), adventitious (derived from experience), or innate (impressed upon the soul by God). You can see where the ideas of the unicorn, the tree, and God all fit. But how do degrees of mental reality fit with mental knowledge as foundational, or with the foundations of knowledge as the essence of reality? And how does all this fit with Descartes' mechanistic concept of causality?

The dualism of body and mind

Descartes' bold answer is that there are two kinds, or realms, of reality. One (the physical) has it as its nature to be extended in space: the other (the mental) has it as its nature to be present to consciousness. Each realm exhibits degrees of reality (which neatly correspond). Both realms are real – the realm of mind-stuff is every bit as real as the realm of matter-stuff. Our knowledge of the mental realm has priority, Descartes believes, without either privileging or impugning its reality.

In short, Descartes solves his problems by a dualism of realities, one mental and the other material. Human beings exist simultaneously on two planes. Gilbert Ryle (1900–1976), who objected strenuously to all this, called it

Descartes' proof that the soul is not material:

'I saw that while I could pretend that I had no body and that there was no world and no place for me to be in, I could not for all that pretend that I did not exist. From this I knew that I was a substance whose essence or nature is to think, something which does not require any place or any material thing in order to exist. So this "I" – that is, the soul which makes me what I am – is completely distinct from the body, is easier to know than the body, and would not fail to be what it is even if the body did not exist.' *Discourse on Method* (1637)

Descartes' dualism of mind and matter:

'... extension in length, breadth and depth constitutes the nature of corporeal substance; and thought constitutes the nature of thinking substance.' *Principles of Philosophy* (1644)

T. H. Huxley on mind/body interaction:

'All the changes of matter being modes of motion, the difficulty of understanding how a moving extended material body was to affect a thinking thing which had no dimension, was as great as that involved in solving the problem of how to hit a nominative case with a stick.' *Hume* (1881)

the dogma of the ghost in the machine – and the practical result of Descartes' dualism (in medicine for example) is indeed a divided human being.

Sophisticated forms of dualism about mind and body still have defenders today. We may not wish to agree with Descartes that there are two quite different sorts of stuff or *substance* in the world, but many people are still attracted by the idea that there is one kind of substance with two quite different sorts of *properties*. And this should be no surprise: mind/body dualism, in its various forms, answers directly to our intuitions about the equal reality, and the fundamental differentness, of thought and matter. A mental image of the Sydney Opera House seems completely real to its experiencer, and yet something quite different in kind from the concrete of the original.

However, the best minds of Descartes' age were soon at work on his substance-dualism. Couldn't something extended think (a brain for example, or – as we might now ask – a computer)? And if not, how does Descartes know that? Then again, how could something extended affect something of an entirely different nature, such as thought (as it seems to when a tree produces an idea of a tree in an observer's mind)? Contrariwise, how could thought influence something of an entirely different nature, such as matter (as it seems to when a decision leads to the movement of an arm or leg)?

One of Descartes' correspondents, Princess Elisabeth, pointedly asked '. . . how man's soul, being only a thinking substance, can determine animal spirits [that is nerve impulses] so as to cause voluntary actions . . . [since] . . . contact seems to me incompatible with something which is immaterial.'

Descartes, however, had additional reasons for defending dualism. If the mind, the essential personality, is something of a quite different nature from the body, then it's easier to believe that the essential person might survive the destruction of the body. For a good Christian like Descartes, the mystery of mind/body interaction has its uses. He replied to Princess Elisabeth that God has provided us with an innate idea of contactless influence. This innate idea was at that time being employed – wrongly, Descartes thought – to explain how the earth's gravity can act on the moon without contact between the two. It should be employed instead, according to Descartes, to explain the interaction of mind and body.

So there you have it. The mind influences the body and vice versa, though they are of entirely different natures. What's strange about that?

Influence without contact

The idea of contactless influence haunts us still. On the one hand, a particle moves because a force acts on it, and on the other, the action of a force (such as the force of gravity) is explained as the exchange of particles (such as 'gravitons').

We seem to have two competing intuitions – that a force needs a mediator (because a genuinely contactless influence would be mere inexplicable correlation), and that any mediator must be driven by a force. And this works – as long as we keep finding smaller mediators and more esoteric forces. But at some point, the mediators will cross the interesting line between 'real entity' and 'useful fiction', and we will either have some real forces mediated by no real particles (or waves or wave-packets), or alternatively, some real particles which move without being driven by any real force.

Well, if we have to choose between movement without force, and force without (intervening) movement – if we can't find another vocabulary such as superstrings or quantum fields – then I expect we'll choose force without intervening movement. In other words, contactless influence.

Do you agree . . . ?

1. **We know our own minds better than anything else.**

   _____

2. **The mind is a parallel reality.**

   _____

3. **Mental decisions cause physical actions.**

   _____

4. **We have an innate idea of contactless influence.**

   _____

CHAPTER 6

Other
People

Chapter 5 set out one problem for Descartes' new
dualistic theory of reality, the problem of
understanding how causal relations between mind
and body are possible. The present chapter sets
out a second problem – the problem of justifying
our belief that other people have a mental life –
and ends by introducing a third.

Descartes – and this is no coincidence – believed another funny thing. He
thought that animals are not conscious. Kick a dog and it will howl – and that's
all there is to it. Kick a human being and he or she will *feel pain* and howl.

Descartes thought this because he thought that only human beings have
minds. Many people suppose that only human beings *reason*, but Descartes
redefined what it is to have a mind (which is a neat trick if you can do it). He
put consciousness centre stage. To have a mind is to be conscious, to know
that you are thinking. So if animals don't think (because they don't speak) and
therefore don't have minds, they don't have consciousness.

It wasn't long before somebody (Julien Offroy de La Mettrie, 1709–1751)
reckoned that human beings are really only animals after all – biological
machines. So perhaps *human beings* have nothing going on up top either. Of
course, they do speak, and reply appropriately to questioning. But if howling
doesn't show a mental life, why should speaking? An automaton of sufficient
sophistication could speak, and appropriately too, without ever thinking so
much as a single thought.

Other minds?

Frightening stuff. If what I really know best is my own mental life, and next
the existence of God very roughly as I conceive of Him, and next the existence
of the external world more or less as I perceive it, then it begins to look as if
the existence of other people's mental lives is a pretty distant hypothesis.
Within Descartes' dualistic point of view, what allows me to be so sure that the
people I meet and speak to every day have a mental life like mine? Shouldn't
this be, at most, a tentative conjecture?

It gets worse. I said (in Chapter 2) that an empiricist thinks our concepts
must come to us from experience. Bishop Berkeley (1685–1753), for example,
says 'I approve of this axiom . . . *nihil est in intellectu quod non prius fuit in
sensu*' (the understanding contains nothing which was not given by the
senses). Well, I never see or hear or have any other kind of experience of other
people's mental lives. Indeed, I never could. Anything I experience must be

Solipsism

The theory that only I exist is called Solipsism. Bertrand Russell (1872–1970) claimed to have received a letter from a logician in which she asserted that she was a solipsist – and was surprised that more people did not take the same view.

Someone who did take at least a similar view was Arthur Schopenhauer (1788–1860). In the same paradoxical vein, he wrote:

'"The world is my representation" is ... a proposition which everyone must recognise as true as soon as he understands it.' *The World as Will and Representation* (1818)

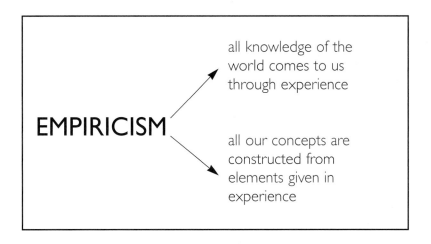

EMPIRICISM

all knowledge of the world comes to us through experience

all our concepts are constructed from elements given in experience

Bertrand Russell put the second, more radical, empiricist claim like this:

'Every proposition which we can understand must be composed wholly of constituents with which we are acquainted.'

part of *my* mental life. So nothing in my experience could give me the concept of another person's experience, and without the concept I can't attach meaning to the phrase 'another person's experience'. It seems to follow that I don't so much as *understand the claim* that other people have a mental life.

In the last chapter, we looked at the problem of interactionism for mind/body dualism – how do mind and body interact if they're as different as Descartes says? One response was the Cartesian shrug: we just can understand this, and they just do. Another response was Leibniz' view that mind and body are like two perfectly synchronised clocks. It *looks* as if they influence each other (because events in the two realms are timed to coincide), but in fact, each goes its own sweet way. In this chapter, however, we are concentrating on an even more serious problem: how do I know that other people have minds? (And for the more radical empiricist, how do I even understand any claim based on this idea, such as 'Betty decided to leave'?)

The argument from analogy

The most popular solution to the knowledge problem (assuming that the understanding problem can be solved somehow), has been the 'argument from analogy'. The idea is very simple. I can correlate in my own case certain outward signs with certain mental events – groans and grimaces with pains for example. I know from bitter experience that when I have a pain I tend to groan and grimace. So when I see the same outward signs in other people, I can reasonably suppose that similar effects (their groans and grimaces being similar to mine) have similar causes (events in a mental life similar to mine). After all, there's clearly an analogy between us in behaviour and general physiology – why not in mental life too?

One problem with this appealing argument is that the numbers are all against it. When we come across a new apple we are justified in supposing it will have pips, because we've had experience of lots of apples which have all had pips. Suppose we'd only ever experienced one apple. How confident could we be that the second apple in our experience would have pips? We might hazard a guess that it would, especially if, in addition to surface similarities, it came from the same tree and had grown in the same way. But after all, the one apple we have examined could be untypical. For all we know, pips could be an aberration. Now suppose someone showed us a barn containing five billion apples and (still allowing us to examine only one) asked us how much we would bet that they *all* had pips. It wouldn't be much, would it?

So the argument from analogy could at best give us very slender evidence that other people have a mental life, and that's not good enough. We are absolutely certain that they do, and to doubt it (or attach as low a probability to it as the argument from analogy suggests) is only one step from barking mad.

Empiricism about meaning

Notice that the second, radical kind of empiricism appears to follow from the first, common-sense kind. If all our knowledge comes through the senses, and our knowledge of language is knowledge, then our knowledge of language (that is, of the meanings of words and sentences) must come through the senses too.

This in turn seems to imply that the meaning of a word could not 'go beyond' our sensory evidence. The word 'infinity' for example, could not mean an infinitely large quantity, since we don't and couldn't experience that. It must therefore mean a constant possibility of adding more.

Unfortunately, lots of our words do in fact seem to 'go beyond' anything we could experience. For example, the whole past tense is in danger since we can't (now or in future) experience the past.

Here's John Stuart Mill (1806–1873) proving that other people have a mental life:

'I conclude that other human beings have feelings like me, because, first, they have bodies like me, which I know, in my own case, to be the antecedent condition of feelings; and because, secondly, they exhibit the acts, and other outward signs, which in my own case I know by experience to be caused by feelings. I am conscious in myself of a series of facts connected by a uniform sequence, of which the beginning is modifications of my body, the middle is feelings, the end is outward demeanour. In the case of other human beings I have the evidence of my senses for the first and last links of the series, but not for the intermediate link . . . In my own case I know that the first link produces the last through the intermediate link, and could not produce it without. Experience, therefore, obliges me to conclude that there must be an intermediate link . . .' *An Examination of Sir William Hamilton's Philosophy* (1865)

And there's another problem. I can *check* that any given apple has pips. I can open it up and look. But how can I check that other people have a mental life? Even if it was all right to open them up, what would I be looking for? But if I can't check that other people have a mental life, if no test or experiment could possibly establish it, what's the point of saying that they do?

So far, we've been looking at the epistemological problems (that is, problems relating to knowledge) arising from Descartes' mind/body dualism. How can I know anything, at least with the kind of certainty I need, about other people's mental realms? Everything going on in other people's minds seems in principle beyond direct access for me. And how can I infer, indirectly, to something which I cannot *in principle* check directly? What's the point of an inference I cannot possibly check?

Well, that's one area of difficulty. Here's another. Descartes thought that since it is the nature of physical reality to take up space, it's impossible for there to be empty space. Nature, as the proverb has it, abhors a vacuum. This has Truly Awful Consequences. If physical reality (which includes our arms, legs, vocal chords and everything else) operates by transmission of impulse, and if all physical phenomena are connected by this system of transmission, then *everything* is caused. For Aristotle, some things have causes, in the important sense of purpose or natural function, and some things (for all practical purposes) don't. For Descartes, however, everything in the material world is hemmed in on every side by particles transmitting impulses: *everything* is subject to mechanical causality.

A universal machine

Now Descartes was wrong about nature abhorring a vacuum – or right, if we count the 'virtual' particles of quantum physics – but the effect of his rejection of Aristotelian causes-as-purposes was to make causality all-encompassing. It's true that, in Descartes' system, God and the mind could cause physical events, and for a time, this non-physical interference hid the dreadful implications. But as we saw, causal interaction between mind and body was always problematic. And before too long, Pierre Simon de Laplace (1749–1827) could say, in reply to Napoleon's inquiry about God's role in Newtonian astronomy, that we have no need of 'that hypothesis'. So if God and the mind have no causal influence after all, it follows that every physical event is caused by other physical events.

There's no escape. Every action, every word, every synapse that fires in your brain, is the result of rigorous material causation. Everything you say, everything you do, everything your brain accomplishes – all inevitable. So not free. So not to be counted either to your merit or your demerit. La Mettrie was right – you *are* an automaton after all.

Descartes on the impossibility of empty space:

'...we very clearly understand that matter whose nature consists simply in its being an extended substance already occupies all the imaginable space in which the alleged additional worlds would have to be located; and we cannot find within us an idea of any other sort of matter.'
Principles of Philosophy (1644)

Laplace on the mechanistic universe:

'We must therefore regard the present state of the universe as an effect of the preceding state and as the cause of the state which is to follow. An intelligence which knew in a single instant all the forces which animate the natural world, and the situations of all the beings that made it up, could, provided it was vast enough to analyse this data, produce a single formula which specified all the movements in the universe from those of the largest bodies to those of the lightest atom. For such an intelligence, nothing would be uncertain, and the future, like the past, would be present before its eyes.'
A Philosophical Essay on Probabilities (1814)

Do you agree . . . ?

1. **Believing that other people have experiences like our own is just an act of faith.**

2. **Animals are just biological machines.**

3. **All our understanding of language comes from experience.**

4. **It's impossible for me to experience someone else's experiences.**

CHAPTER 7

Universal Causality

> This chapter illustrates the far-reaching consequences of the change from cause-as-purpose to cause-as-impulse. If *everything* is caused (in the sense of mechanically produced by the transmission of impulse), can any of our actions be called free?

So far, I've been writing the 'great man' kind of history (of ideas). I don't need to tell you that that's nonsense, of course. To take one example, Descartes was not the only writer, or the first, to outlaw final causes from scientific explanation. The list includes Ramus, Sanches, Galileo, van Helmont, Bacon and Hobbes – and many others were tacit partners in this cultural revolution. It was not something which one person, however great, could possibly accomplish alone. So why do I say, misleadingly, 'Descartes established this' or 'Descartes introduced that'? I'm afraid it's simply one of the penalties of brevity. Another, probably worse, is the 'big idea' illusion. Hume said causality is only constant conjunction? Yes he did, but Malebranche (1638–1715) had said something similar, and others before him. In Malebranche, the big idea (that one thing never *makes* another happen) is essentially a religious point: only God has causal power. In Hume, the 'same' big idea is a consequence of, and stimulant to, empiricism. So it's misleading and wrong to speak as if ideas can be sealed off from each other and examined separately. I do it, and will continue to do it, hoping to demonstrate the importance of these big ideas, and to introduce the people who gave them their fullest and best (if not their first) expression. Sharper focus – on both people and ideas – has to be paid for with narrower scope.

Loeb and Leopold

Our big idea for this chapter is determinism. Here's an illustration of its importance. One summer day, in Chicago, two rich boys hired a car, drove around for a while, then picked up a younger friend who was on his way home from school. The two had decided to murder somebody, but they hadn't quite decided who. The main instigator of the plot, Richard, hit the boy they had picked up over the head with a chisel, pulled the fresh corpse, which was bleeding copiously, into the back seat and wrapped a blanket round it. Then they drove around their neighbourhood for a while, before taking the body out of town, stripping it to prevent identification, and dumping it twenty

Francis Bacon, for example, wrote:

'. . . causes . . . are not improperly divided into four kinds: the material, the formal, the efficient and the final. But of these the final cause rather corrupts than advances the sciences, except such as have to do with human action.' *Novum Organum* (1620)

Pierre Gassendi (1592–1655) sharply attacked Aristotelian science:

'. . . there are many things that can be known, but not . . . by an Aristotelian science: only by an experimental science or one following appearances.' *Paradoxes Against the Aristotelians* (1624)

miles south of the city. This done, they drove back into Chicago, had dinner in a restaurant, drove on to the home of the other boy, Nathan (leaving the incriminating car parked outside), and sat up till late going over the exciting events of the day. Next morning, they cleaned up the car – very imperfectly – returned it to the car hire firm, and went about their business.

Naturally, they were caught. One of them had dropped a pair of distinctive horn-rimmed glasses where they left the body. When challenged, their concocted story quickly broke and they confessed.

Two elements contributed to the ensuing sensation. First, the boys had no apparent motive for the killing. They said they had done it for the experience. Second, the boys (like their victim) came from extremely wealthy families, and many people feared that their parents would hire expensive lawyers who would get them off. The whole case was widely publicised and the chance of finding an unprejudiced juror was effectively nil.

The great liberal lawyer Clarence Darrow took the case, in order to fight the clamour from every side that the boys should hang. He advised the boys to plead guilty, which they did, so that no jury would be required. He also arranged for his fee to be fixed by a neutral arbitrator.

Darrow's argument was that the boys had been able to plan and commit the murder because they were psychologically abnormal, that they were not responsible for this abnormality (because it was a result of genetic or educational factors beyond their control), and that because they were not responsible, they could not be punished. Society should certainly be protected from them, but they should not be executed.

Darrow arranged for several psychologists (then called 'alienists') to interview the boys in order to establish their abnormality. The alienists agreed that the boys were strangely lacking in normal emotional reactions, and gave evidence to that effect. In his long closing speech for the defence, Darrow emphasised the likely causes of this emotional deficit. One boy had had a very intensive education with little parental contact: the other (Darrow speculated) must have inherited some faulty gene from some more or less distant ancestor. At any rate, whatever the cause of their condition might be, the boys themselves were not responsible for it, and therefore could not be blamed.

Darrow's closing speech

Here are some extracts from Darrow's closing speech for the defence:

> I know that one of two things happened to Richard Loeb: that this terrible crime was inherent in his organism, and came from some ancestor; or that it came through his education and training after he was born . . .

Clarence Darrow

Isaiah Berlin (1909–1997) on the impact of determinism:

'If social and psychological determinism were established as an accepted truth, our world would be transformed more radically than was the teleological world of the classical and middle ages by the triumphs of mechanistic principles or those of natural selection. Our words – our modes of speech and thought – would be transformed in literally unimaginable ways.' *Four Essays on Liberty* (1969)

I do not know what remote ancestors may have sent down the seed that corrupted him, and I do not know through how many ancestors it may have passed until it reached Dickie Loeb. All I know is that it is true and there is not a biologist in the world who will not say that I am right.

I know, Your Honor, that every atom of life in all this universe is bound up together. I know that a pebble cannot be thrown into the ocean without disturbing every drop of water in the sea . . . I know that every influence, conscious and unconscious, acts and reacts on every living organism, and that no one can fix the blame.

Nature is strong and she is pitiless. She works in her own mysterious way, and we are her victims. We have not much to do with it ourselves . . . What had this boy to do with it? He was not his own father; he was not his own mother; he was not his own grandparents . . . He did not make himself. And yet he is to be compelled to pay.

Is Dickie Loeb to blame because out of the infinite forces that conspired to form him, the infinite forces that were at work producing him ages before he was born, that because out of these infinite combinations he was born without [an emotional system and emotional reactions]? . . . Is he to blame that his machine is imperfect?

Still we go on, as if human conduct was not influenced and controlled by natural laws the same as all the rest of the universe is the subject of law. We treat crime as if it had no cause . . . It never occurs to the lawyer that crime has a cause as certainly as disease, and that the way to treat any abnormal condition rationally is to remove the cause.

I can hardly imagine that we are in the twentieth century. And yet there are men who seriously say that for what nature has done, for what life has done, for what training has done, you should hang these boys.

In addition to this powerful deterministic argument, Darrow had another, legal argument against the death penalty. In the preceding ten years, only one man out of the four hundred and fifty who had pled guilty to murder in the city of Chicago had been executed, and he had been forty years old (the boys were eighteen and seventeen at the time of the murder). Fortified by these arguments, the judge managed to resist intense media pressure for execution. Richard Loeb and Nathan Leopold were sentenced to life imprisonment.

This case inspired at least two films. This scene from the Orson Welles film *Compulsion* shows public reaction to the murder.

Kant (1724–1804) on determinism:

'Philosophy must assume that no real contradiction will be found between the freedom and the physical necessity of the same human actions, because it cannot give up the conception of nature any more than that of freedom.' *Fundamental Principles of the Metaphysic of Morals* (1785)

But something's wrong here. If determinism applies, it applies universally. It doesn't apply to criminals and not to judges. It doesn't apply to bad childhoods and not good ones, or to abnormal psyches and not normal ones. What could Darrow say, then, if the judge had replied, 'Your clients may indeed have been unable to avoid the actions which brought them to this trial. But by the same deterministic principles, I am unable to avoid a verdict of guilty, and given my background, equally unable to avoid a sentence of death'?

Two kinds of unfreedom

It's worth noticing that determinism can be stated in physiological, or in pyschological, terms. *Physiological* determinism holds that the system of nerve impulses, brain processes, glandular activity etc. is a system which, though enormously complicated, is no more free than, for example, the dripping of a tap. The alternative – perhaps abandoning the firings of neurons and the molecular action of neuro-transmitters as too complex – is to state determinism in terms of wishes, decisions, perceptions of self-interest, influences from childhood, and so on. This *psychological* determinism deals in mental events and resulting actions, not brain events and resulting bodily movements.

Do you agree . . . ?

1. **Loeb and Leopold deserved to hang.**

   _____

2. **We are not responsible for anything we are caused to do.**

   _____

3. **'A pebble cannot be thrown into the ocean without disturbing every drop of water in the sea.'**

   _____

4. **Darrow was determined to believe in determinism, and so his belief was an irrational compulsion.**

   _____

CHAPTER 8

Freedom

This chapter continues the discussion of determinism, first by distinguishing it from two other related problems, and then by explaining one proposed solution. According to this proposed solution, we are free when we are not prevented from doing what we want.

Perhaps the first thing to do in discussing determinism is to distinguish it from two other problems, equally inimical to human freedom. The first is fatalism and the second is predestination.

Fatalism can be summed up in the slogan: whatever will be, will be. If something is going to happen, then it *really is* going to happen. And if it really is going to happen, then there's nothing we can do to stop it.

What's wrong with this short, bewitching argument? Well, *perhaps* there's some sort of shift of meaning in the 'really is' parts. At first 'really is' corresponds to the 'necessarily' in '*Necessarily, if something is going to happen, then it's going to happen*'. But in the next sentence, it somehow comes to mean that the event in question is going to happen *no matter what*. Has there been a subtle change of meaning here, from a necessity applying to a process of inference (if p, then p), to a necessity applying to a real-world event? To say that *if* x is going to happen, then x is going to happen, is not at all to say that x *is* going to happen.

However, that point may not be enough to defuse the argument. Several twentieth-century philosophers have argued in favour of Aristotle's more radical suggestion, that propositions about specific future events are neither true nor false. They're guesses or predictions which *come* true when the event in question happens.

The second problem which isn't determinism is predestination. For Christians, God is omniscient. But if God knows everything, He knows the future too. So He knows that, as it might be, my soul will go to heaven when I die. But if God knows it, it must be so: my soul certainly *will* go to heaven. But if my soul certainly will go to heaven, why should I bother to be good? James Hogg's splendid novel *The Confessions of a Justified Sinner* explores the human consequences of exactly this line of thought.

Historically, the most popular response to this problem has been to deny that God knows what's going to happen *in advance* of its happening. To say that God knows what's going to happen before it happens involves placing God in the onward flow of time. But according to the popular response, God exists outside of time.

Aristotle on fatalism:

'Everything necessarily is or is not, and will be or will not be; but one cannot divide and say that one or the other is necessary. I mean, for example: it is necessary that there either will be or will not be a sea-battle tomorrow, but it is not necessary that a sea-battle will take place tomorrow, nor necessary that one will not . . . It is necessary for one or the other of the contradictories to be true or false – not, however, this one or that one . . . [It is necessary] for one to be true rather than the other, but not *already* true or false.' *De Interpretatione* (date uncertain)

In this rather cryptic passage, Aristotle seems to make two points. First, that 'Necessarily, X or Y' does not imply 'Necessarily X, or necessarily Y'. And second, that a statement which will be true or false tomorrow might be neither true nor false today. We still aren't entirely sure if the first point is enough to defuse the problem of fatalism, or if the second (which has problems of its own) is also needed.

Distinguishing God's eternal life from just going on forever, the Roman philosopher Boethius (c.480–524) said:

'Eternity is the complete and total possession of unending life all at once.' *The Consolations of Philosophy* (524)

In other words, eternal life is not just more years: it's something which makes the whole idea of a 'year' or any other measure of time obsolete.

Another response is to suspect a subtle change of meaning in the words 'must' and 'certainly' in the statement of the problem. Our present concern, however, is with the threat to free action from determinism, not the threats from divine foreknowledge or the future tense.

The meaning of freedom

Notice first of all that freedom is not only essential to moral responsibility (a point we'll explore in the next chapter). It's also presupposed by various non-moral feelings, such as frustration, disappointment, resentment, and on the positive side, self-confidence, hope, ambition. All these and many other feelings take it for granted that our efforts, which we can at will apply or withold, make a difference. More circuitously, scientific procedure also assumes that we are free. The scientist devises a theory or sets up an experiment in a *rational* response to the existing evidence. If the theory and the experiment are as inevitable as clockwork, there's no sense in which either can be reasonable or good. What is the point of trying to evaluate them in these ways when their production and reception are determined?

So if freedom is in the end untenable, we don't just lose the ability to praise and blame in moral matters, we lose almost everything we currently recognise as human life. As Augustine (354–430) said, discussing Cicero (106–43BC), without freedom 'the whole organisation of human life is subverted.'

The most popular response to the problem of determinism has been to define freedom negatively. According to Hobbes (opposite), freedom means absence of constraint. It means not being prevented from doing what you want to do. If your hands are tied, or if someone has a gun to your head, or if you're under post-hypnotic suggestion, then your actions are constrained in different ways. In these cases, you are not free and so not morally responsible.

The popular response, then, has been to argue that determinism doesn't stop you doing what you want to do. On the contrary, say some enthusiasts for this line, it *allows* you to do what you want to do. If your actions did not affect the world in reliable ways (thanks to universal causation) the whole notion of action would be impossible. More importantly, since determinism is no constraint, we have the freedom which we need for moral responsibility and the rest. According to Hobbes and his modern followers, there's really no problem about determinism.

The short riposte to this 'compatibilist' line (determinism is compatible with freedom because the only freedom we need is absence of constraint) is that it gives us only the freedom of water to run downhill, or of clockwork to unwind – not a very human kind of freedom, it would seem. *Real* freedom,

Positive and negative freedom

In a seventeenth-century debate between Thomas Hobbes (1588–1679) and Bishop John Bramhall, Hobbes argued that negative freedom is all we need (so determinism is not a problem). Bramhall contended for the importance of positive freedom:

Hobbes: '. . . he is free to do a thing who may do it if he have the will to do it, and may forbear if he have the will to forbear.'

Bramhall: '. . . true liberty consists in the elective power of the rational will . . . Reason is the root, the fountain, the origin of true liberty.'

Hobbes: 'I do not understand how reason can be the root of true liberty, if the Bishop, as he says in the beginning, had the liberty to write this discourse.'

Bramhall: 'He that cannot understand the difference between *free to do if he will*, and *free to will*, is not fit, as I have said in the stating of the question, to hear this controversy disputed, much less to be a writer in it.'

Debate in the seventeeth century was nothing if not robust.

A definition of freedom by Bertrand Russell:

'Freedom in general may be defined as the absence of obstacles to the realisation of desires.'

Freedom here is primarily negative, but the word 'desires' could in turn be defined so as to give more emphasis to positive freedom.

many people feel, must involve some motivation which fully belongs to the agent. A genuinely free action must spring from a reason which is genuinely *my* reason. If an action springs from peer pressure, or the influence of advertising, or from self-deception, then it is not free in any positive sense (and this was Bramhall's point). It may be unhindered, but that doesn't mean it's free.

Positive freedom?

It's hard to make this idea of positive freedom at all precise, and yet mere absence of constraint does seem a rather unsatisfactory notion of freedom. A more recent attempt to articulate the feeling that human freedom must be something more than absence of constraint turns on the idea of being able to do otherwise. When someone does something freely, we seem to suppose that he or she could have done something else instead. But this 'could have done otherwise' seems to be incompatible with determinism, since determinism says that given the existing conditions, only what did happen could have happened. Does this capture the conflict we intuitively feel between freedom and determinism?

Not at all, says the compatibilist. When we say that someone could have done otherwise, we mean (says the compatibilist) that he or she could have done otherwise *if he or she had wanted or decided to*. We don't mean that he or she could have done otherwise if everything else had stayed just the same. The latter would indeed be ruled out by determinism, but the former is perfectly compatible with it. If there is a change in the prior conditions (such as a change in what the agent wants or decides to do), determinism in fact insists that things *would* have turned out differently.

One question this raises is whether wants or decisions (and other mental events) are really suitable candidates for the kind of causal explanation trumpeted by determinism. When we say 'He took his umbrella because the road was wet', is that the *same* kind of 'because' as in 'The car skidded because the road was wet'? You might say that the first gives a reason and the second gives a cause, but then, are reasons causes? And if not, how do they influence actions?

A more immediate question, however, is this: is it true to say that 'He could have done otherwise' means the same as 'He would have done otherwise if he had wanted/decided to'? I don't think it does mean the same, but I'm afraid I don't have any nice knock-down arguments to prove I'm right. I also don't think that reasons are the right sort of thing to be causes, but again, sadly, I don't have a short explanation of why not.

Thomas Reid (1710–1796) on motives and causes:

'I grant that all rational beings are influenced, and ought to be influenced, by motives. But the relation between a motive and the action is of a very different nature from the relation between an efficient cause and its effect. An efficient cause must be a being that exists, and has power to produce the effect. A motive is not a thing that exists. It is only a thing conceived in the mind of the agent. Motives supply liberty in the agent, otherwise they have no influence at all.' (unpublished manuscript)

F. H. Bradley (1846–1924) on freedom:

'Freedom means *chance*; you are free, because there is no reason which will account for your particular acts, because no one in the world, not even yourself, can possibly say what you will, or will not, do next. You are "accountable", in short, because you are a wholly "unaccountable" creature.' *Ethical Studies* (1876)

Conclusion

So what can we say by way of summary here? There has been a clear historical sequence, from worries about fatalism, to worries about predestination, to worries about determinism. We began to worry *seriously* about determinism only two or three centuries ago. So perhaps it's not surprising that we're still confused about it. It's also an issue which is very deeply interwoven with our concept of ourselves, and our concept of the world (which may indeed contain both chaotic and probabilistic systems, but which nevertheless has no room, it seems, for a free 'could have done otherwise'). On the one hand, we have an image of human agents acting according to their own freely developed purposes: on the other, an image of the natural world devoid of purpose, governed by causality. We fundamentally need both, and yet they seem to conflict with each other.

Problems at this depth, and with this degree of entanglement with other problems, just *are* difficult to deal with. I don't despair of progress even here, but I don't expect it to happen overnight.

Identities?

Compare the following three statements:

1. A series of muscular contractions drew the ink-dispenser in a complicated series of curves across the page.

2. He signed his name.

3. He pardoned the condemned man.

The very same event might be described in these three ways, and this seems to imply that if the event is fully determined under description 1, it's also fully determined under descriptions 2 and 3.

But does that really follow? Perhaps the 'higher-level' descriptions remove the basic event from the realm of causal explanation. For example, it makes sense to ask for the mathematical equation which specifies the series of curves. But it makes no sense at all to ask for the mathematical specification of a pardon.

Do you agree . . . ?

1. **Whatever will be, will be.**

2. **Determinism is as dangerous to science as it is to morality.**

3. **The only kind of freedom we need is absence of constraint.**

4. **'She could have helped with the envelopes' means 'She would have helped with the envelopes if she had wanted to.'**

CHAPTER 9

Temptation

In the present chapter, we see two further consequences of causes-as-impulses. First, if purposes are not causes, then they cannot really account for actions. Second, if morality cannot be understood as a struggle between 'higher' purposes and the causal influences of 'lower' drives and appetites, it must be only a matter of calculated self-interest.

It's natural to suppose that if we are free anywhere, we are free in what we think. Well, that's not false, but it isn't the whole truth either. We also have thoughts – such as painful memories – which come whether we want them or not. It sometimes happens that one thought leads to another in a way which seems almost mechanical. And of course, emotional responses are even less under our control. We feel sad or angry or amused without *choosing* to do so. The point of calling these things passions was that we are more or less passive in experiencing them.

So, some of our mental life seems relatively controllable, and some less so. Some of it seems to follow at our bidding, and some seems to happen by itself. Do the controllable and the spontaneous kinds of thinking lead equally to action? On reflection, it seems that the controllable kind of thinking cannot be the real source of any action. If I choose to think about whether there are eggs in the fridge, for example, that is itself a kind of (mental) action. I could have done otherwise. But if controllable thinking results from a choice or decision in this way, and so counts as a kind of action, then although it can in turn lead to a physical action, such as opening the fridge door, it seems to be only the intermediate source of that action. The real source is, for example, the (involuntary) feeling of hunger which led me to think that an omelette would be nice, which led me to wonder whether there were eggs in the fridge.

The slave of the passions

Considerations of this kind led Hume to the view – shocking at least to Enlightenment sensibilities – that 'Reason is and ought only to be the slave of the passions'. In fact, whereas I've been allowing that the controllable kinds of thinking might be an 'intermediate source' of action, for Hume, Reason has no motive power whatsoever. He argues that a person could reason through the same series of thoughts, whatever they are, and do nothing at all, if he or she didn't *feel* strongly about the events envisioned. According to Hume, controllable Reason can only work out the best way to get what the less

Are actions caused by drives . . .

The term 'drive' was coined in 1918 – only six years before Darrow defended Loeb and Leopold – and for the next three decades, psychologists made determined efforts to explain as much of human behaviour as possible in terms of drives. In addition to the obvious candidates – drives for food, warmth and sex – drives for achievement, affection, knowledge, respect, self-actualisation and various other things were postulated. Freud's Eros and Thanatos instincts are essentially drives. In the early forties, Clark Hull proposed drive theories of action and learning: to put it very simply, more drive means more activity and less drive means less learning.

The fundamental problem for the drive programme, and the reason it has now fallen from favour, is that we have no secure way to identify drive states independently of the behaviour they're supposed to cause. A cause which cannot be identified independently of its alleged effects is – always – a snare and a delusion.

. . . or explained by purposes?

It can of course be argued that we *have* to see others as purposive. The cognitive psychologist Michael Tomasello has recently claimed that, beginning at nine months or so, human babies begin to see other people as following purposes of their own (see *The Cultural Origins of Human Cognition,* 1999). They begin, for example, to *share* attention to objects, in ways which chimpanzees in the wild never do. Tomasello argues that adopting this stance towards others is necessary for language learning and for cultural development. Severely autistic children don't learn language, on this view, because they don't see others as *intending* to communicate with them.

Notice that this makes the argument from analogy (Chapter 6) work harder than ever. Babies are represented here as generalising from their own experience of purposive action, to the belief that other people also act purposively.

controllable Will happens to want. By itself, it can't produce the lifting of a little finger.

So those purposes of action which we consciously adopt – like the sculptor's decision to display a statue at the festival – cannot be the real source of any action. The real source must be some kind of drive or motive which was not freely adopted, which was simply *there*, like the sculptor's drive for recognition perhaps. To put it very simply, if purposes aren't really causes, then they can't have any power to produce actions. Our actions must be produced by something else, and this seems in the end to commit us to seeing other people as 'driven', not essentially purposive at all. The seventeenth-century decision to do without final causes throws a long shadow over the explanations we now give of things we do.

I presented determinism (at the end of Chapter 6) as arising from Descartes' vision of a universe completely filled with matter. The problem was that if every physical change is caused by impulses from the surrounding particles of matter, then those physical changes which are our actions seem to be constrained. If Amy pushes Belinda into Charlotte, Belinda is not to be blamed, because her movements resulting from the push were not free actions. So if material impulses are just (much) smaller pushes, and if they determine all our actions, it seems to follow that no action we perform is free.

However, if causes are not impulses but correlations, this version of the problem disappears. Correlations don't push. Unfortunately, a new version of the problem rises to replace the old. If we have outlawed final causes, they cannot figure in the correlations which constitute, according to Hume, the only kind of cause. The new version of the problem of determinism, therefore, is that the only legitimate kind of explanation has no place for purposes, including human purposes in acting. The agent's purposes in acting – *our reasons* for doing the things we do – are excluded by methodological fiat.

This means that doing without final causes affects moral evaluation, not just at the level invoked by Darrow, of 'constrained, therefore not punishable', but at the deeper level of 'not acting from reasons at all, therefore not moral'. And if this is right, the compatibilist attempt to rescue *freedom* misses the real point: what needs rescuing is *purpose*. I said in the last chapter that determinism (of whichever kind) would affect all areas of human life, not just morality. Our next task, however, is to bring out the special depth of the connection between final causes and moral thinking.

Doing the right thing

It often happens that people do things while in the grip of some passion, which they are later inclined to regret. One strikes in anger, for example, only

The chariot is an ancient and powerful image of reason harnessing instincts and emotions. Without the horses, the driver goes nowhere: without the driver, the horses go all over the place.

Thomas Hobbes

Hobbes on self-interest:

Hobbes' *Leviathan* (1651) is a wonderfully forthright and single-minded attempt to derive all individual and political action from self-interest. Why would anyone submit to the authority of a ruler? Only because the ruler can then enforce laws which reduce the individual's chances of sudden and violent death. Why do people laugh? Only because something gives them a feeling of sudden superiority, as when someone slips on a banana skin or makes a silly mistake. And so on.

to wish one had restrained the impulse. To a first approximation, then, we can say that morality begins in the conflict between our more controllable and our less controllable thinking, in the war between consciously-developed purposes and spontaneous impulses or drives.

This is a very *rough* first approximation, to be sure. We can certainly have bad purposes, and good impulses. And of course, not all attempts to control the spontaneous parts of our mental life are moral. But at the first approximation level, morality is an attempt to fortify our purposes sufficiently to stand against our impulses. This explains, incidentally, why negative freedom – the mere absence of constraint – seems so unsatisfactory. It ignores this inner conflict in favour of the external struggle to get what we want. The idea of positive freedom is a way of emphasising that morality is about self-control, about taking command of what happens spontaneously in us.

If this is correct, morality is a battleground between the kinds of thinking we can control, and the kinds we can't. And as you might expect, people who have written about morality have tended to take sides. Those siding with control, like Plato and Kant, have emphasised that the controllable kind of thinking represents our higher nature, constituting our uniqueness both as human beings among the animals, and as individuals in our community. Others, like Hume and Rousseau (1712–1778), have stressed our natural goodness and the problems of attempts at control. However, if morality is about self-control, there will obviously be a very serious question about justification. Why *should* we thwart our first inclinations? Why should anyone accept this 'discipline of the emotions'?

The common-sense justification for self-restraint is that something bad will happen to you if you don't. If you strike someone *bigger* than you in anger, you are liable to get a drubbing in return. Even if you strike someone smaller, they may work out a way of getting back at you. Or more insidiously, you may turn into the sort of person who habitually strikes out in anger, later strike at someone bigger because you can't stop yourself, and duly get the drubbing you deserve. In this way, self-interest, if it takes a long-term view, seems to suggest that striking out in anger is not a good idea. Self-interest, then, might seem enough to explain the need to inhibit our spontaneous impulses.

The problem with this is that a self-interested action, even if successful in the long-term, might still be (morally) wrong. Suppose that, one dark night, I find a wallet full of money. No one has seen me find it, and the owner's loss (let's suppose) will not affect me in any way. Let's also suppose that there aren't enough wallets full of money lying around for keeping this one to be habit-forming. Although keeping the wallet is clearly the self-interested thing to do, it's also clearly the *wrong* thing to do.

In the same way, an action which is damaging or even disastrous to the

Is it unreasonable to be unfair?

Suppose you are about to play some sort of game against someone. Your opponent offers you this choice: the game can be played 'flat', using rules which don't favour either side, or 'tilted', using rules which favour one side over the other. You ask who the rules will favour, but that has yet to be decided, and when it is, it will be decided by chance.

Would you rather play the game flat or tilted? The more tilted the rules are, the more the game becomes one of chance, and some people do prefer games of chance over games of skill. But suppose you don't know anything at all about your opponent's ability – he or she may be as good as you, or better, or worse. And suppose your life depends on the outcome. I don't know exactly why, but it seems more reasonable to me to opt for the flat rules. If the rules are tilted against me, I may have no real chance to win: if they're tilted in my favour, winning may be too easy to be interesting. In either case, the point of playing the game is under threat.

According to John Rawls (1921–), an unequal *society*, in which some people are given enormous advantages, is like the tilted game. No reasonable person, insofar as they are reasonable, would choose it.

This game analogy, by the way, does not suggest high income taxes, handicapping success while the game is in progress. It suggests high death duties – as in Japan – to level the playing field for the next generation.

Is it inhuman to be unjust?

In Plato's *Republic*, a repulsive Chalcedonian called Thrasymachus argues that successful injustice is wise and good, and promotes the unjust man's happiness.

Socrates argues in reply that the unjust man sets himself up against everyone, whereas the just man has natural allies in other people who love justice. The unjust man is essentially alone against the world.

Socrates goes on to claim that the unjust man is also divided against *himself*, that he is 'incapable of action because he is not at unity with himself.' This means that injustice is bad because it conflicts with the purpose or natural function of the soul or mind, which is to control action.

I think Socrates would probably have approved of films like *The Treasure of the Sierra Madre* or *Shallow Grave*.

agent's self-interest, might be morally right. Washington's legendary refusal to tell a lie is a case in point. Socrates' respect for the law of Athens cost him his life, even though the verdict which condemned him was (it seems) political. So it looks as if self-interest is one thing, and morality something quite different, and it just so happens that both involve inhibiting first inclinations. Which brings us back to the problem of finding a justification for the *moral* cases of inhibition, an even more urgent problem now, because we've just seen that morality might actually damage self-interest.

One response is to appeal to an 'enlightened' – or at any rate unobvious – self-interest. Religious moralities, for example, can be interpreted in this way. Returning the wallet, telling the painful truth, obeying the law, serve a higher self-interest in that they will get me to heaven, enable me to escape the burden of rebirth, please the ancestors who will then help me in various other matters, and so on. A different way of appealing to unobvious self-interest, which has the advantage of depending on no special beliefs about how things really are, recommends a larger-scale perspective. Given that everyone else is pursuing their self-interest too, we will all maximise our self-interest by accepting various rules as binding upon all, even if those rules occasionally damage our immediate interests. To give a simple (non-moral) example: stopping at a red light is irksome if I'm in a hurry, but overall, it helps me get there if we all follow the rule of stopping at red lights.

To some people, however, even enlightened self-interest is not enough. After all, on this account, if I can break a rule and get away with it (driving through a red light on another dark night, say, when nobody is looking), then that's what I ought to do. On this account, someone who breaks a moral rule and genuinely profits from it deserves only praise. A *successful* thief, or murderer, is morally irreproachable.

Self-interest or human nature?

If this is unacceptable, it seems we have to turn away from self-interest, however enlightened, to the idea of an essential human nature. If moral self-control cannot be justified by what we want, it must be justified by what we *are*. It's worth noticing that religious moralities can also be interpreted in this way. It is because I am essentially a divine breath, or a non-self, or a member of my family line, that immoral action is to be avoided. Doing something morally bad is false to my nature: it is an outrage to what I really am. Secular – or comparatively secular – versions of this kind of morality have appealed to notions of special human intuition (Plato or G. E. Moore), or human reasoning (Locke or Kant), or to concepts of human flourishing (Aristotle) or the human situation (Existentialism), and we'll have a closer look at one of them in Chapter 10.

The prisoner's dilemma

Two men accused of a crime are kept in separate cells. They are offered this deal:

- **confess**, and if the other man does not confess, you will go free. The other man will serve ten years. If the other man also confesses, you will both serve six years.

- **don't confess**, and if the other man confesses, he will go free and you will serve ten years. If he does not confess, you will both serve two years.

What should a selfish individual do? Obviously, a selfish individual should confess. If you confess, you serve either zero or six years. If you don't, you serve either two or ten years.

But if both confess, twelve man-years are spent in prison, the worst result in terms of overall time lost. If both trust the other not to confess, or if both accept as a general principle that there must be honour among thieves, four man-years are spent in prison, the best possible result in terms of overall time lost.

Since many ordinary situations have this 'prisoner's dilemma' structure, it's clear that individual selfishness does not always tend to produce the best results overall. A god who wished humanity to survive would reserve at least a corner of the human heart for trust and principle.

Do you agree . . . ?

1. **Controllable thinking only exists to help satisfy basically uncontrollable drives.**

   _____

2. **If purposes aren't causes they can't produce actions.**

   _____

3. **Morality is essentially a matter of inhibiting what we spontaneously want to do.**

   _____

4. **The fundamental motive of all human action is self-interest.**

   _____

CHAPTER 10

Right and Wrong

In this chapter, we examine Kant's account of morality. This illustrates, first, the importance of purpose or teleology for moral thinking, and second, the conviction that morality must be based, not on any passing inclination or calculation of advantage, but on a free and rational internalisation of duty.

A distinction is often made between consequentialist and deontological (or duty-based) moralities. The first type emphasises the importance of the consequences of an action in deciding whether it is right or wrong: the second type emphasises that some kinds of action are just right (or wrong) regardless of the consequences in any particular case. Utilitarianism – the view that the right thing to do is whichever action most increases happiness, or most reduces suffering – is the most important example of a consequentialist morality. If, on the other hand, we think that breaking a promise or killing a child is *always* wrong, no matter what the consequences, that's deontological.

Well, that's an important distinction, but I've been suggesting another way of dividing up the territory – into moralities which justify self-control in terms of self-*interest* (whether immediate or more distant), and those which turn instead to our essential human *nature*. Self-interest theories have the advantage of appealing to common sense (unless they depend on special beliefs about how things really are). 'Human nature' theories, on the other hand, are able to present us with a higher, and perhaps inspiring, truth about ourselves. They can appeal, not merely to what a given individual happens to want, but to what any human being *ought* to want.

Human nature

I suppose the question of what we essentially *are* holds a certain charm for us, and we do seem in fact to be different in important ways from any other animal. At any rate, various opinions have been advanced. Plato believed that the important thing about human beings is that we have a soul whose elements can be brought into harmony if we live according to justice. Aristotle, as usual more down-to-earth, defined man as a 'politikon zoon', an animal with political institutions. As such, our best condition (*eudaimonia*) results when we follow virtue, by avoiding what are regarded as extremes in our society. Existentialist moralities locate our uniqueness, not in any essence, but in our situation. In the (very) long term, nothing we can do will make the

Utilitarianism

The magic words – 'the greatest happiness of the greatest number' – were probably first put together by Francis Hutcheson, an influence on Hume and Thomas Jefferson. Hutcheson was scolded by the church for teaching the 'false and dangerous doctrine that the standard of moral goodness is the promotion of the happiness of others'.

But utilitarianism was really put to work by Jeremy Bentham (1748–1832), who rigorously applied the test of 'augmenting the happiness of the community' to matters of social policy and law. Bentham was splendidly eccentric, directing that his body should be mummified after death, for the pleasure it might give others to see it. It still sits in University College London, though the head, which didn't mummify well, is made of wax.

Happiness

Utilitarianism is at present the dominant morality for political thinking in the West. Alternatives – such as the view that political action should further the interests of the ruling family, or the spread of a religion, or the greater glory of the state – now seem tenable only to the extent that they promise by these means to increase human happiness.

But what does 'happiness' mean? For Bentham, it meant simple pleasure, a view qualified by Mill's insistence that there are 'higher' pleasures. In fact, the real consensus which underpins the adoption of utilitarianism, is that human happiness consists not for example in service to a ruler, religion or state, but in material well-being, leisure and consumption.

slightest difference – and unlike other animals, *we know it*. According to Nietzsche (1844–1900) and Camus (1913–1960), in their different ways, this is a truth which we can nevertheless embrace with 'joy'.

Big fat books have been written about all of these moralities (and rightly so). Here – of course – we only have time to sketch one theory, and I've chosen Kant's, which locates our uniqueness, and the source of true morality, in the human ability to reason, and in the fact that human beings are ends-in-themselves.

Let's begin with our ability to reason. As rational creatures, we can see that certain actions are self-defeating. I won't save much in bank account A if I spend everything I have in bank account B and instruct my bank to top up B from A as necessary. Anyone who engages in this self-defeating kind of behaviour is acting irrationally – though some cases may be too complex to be anything more than normal human error. Bugs in complex computer programs are self-defeating but not really *irrational*, by normal human standards.

Be reasonable!

Bugs notwithstanding, any rational creature wants to avoid self-defeating actions. Add to this the fact that other people can observe and imitate our actions, and we arrive (Kant argues) at a rule which any rational creature surrounded by possible imitators must endorse. The rule is: avoid any action which, if others were to imitate it, would be self-defeating.

Let's take an example. It's often in a person's interest to tell a lie, and of course, at least some lies will go undetected, and so serve the liar's interest, even in the long term. But if lying were to be generally imitated, no one would believe anything they were told. There would be a breakdown of trust, and in this case telling a lie would not have the desired effect. In other words, telling a lie is a self-defeating action. It's a kind of action which, given that we are surrounded by possible imitators, tends to undermine its own effectiveness.

What this means is that any rational creature surrounded by possible imitators must endorse truth-telling, *not* because telling lies has bad consequences, but simply because he or she is rational. As this example shows, Kant's moral theory is explicitly non-consequentialist: he wants to show that morality can be derived from our nature as rational beings, not from our fear of, or desire for, certain consequences. To emphasise this point, he describes a moral law as a *categorical* imperative, one which does not depend on what we happen to want or fear. A merely *hypothetical* imperative (like 'Turn right at the station') applies, by contrast, only *if* we happen to fear or desire certain consequences.

Kant on duty:

Kant says that there are lots of things which it is morally good to do, even if they cannot be called strict duties. Helping others in distress, for example, is not a strict duty, but it is meritorious.

So is it possible to will the maxim 'Ignore others in distress' as a universal law? It doesn't seem self-defeating in the same way as 'Tell a lie whenever you feel like it'.

Kant argues that we cannot actually want the 'ignoring others' maxim to be followed by everyone, because we know that we ourselves may need help sometime. In this case, we can't will the maxim as a universal law, not because the action would be self-defeating, but because it might rebound to our disadvantage.

What about suicide? Kant thinks we have a strict duty not to commit suicide, and he argues that it is inconsistent to will that the very motives intended to preserve life (desire to avoid pain etc.) should be used to end it. But this again is not exactly self-defeating.

The truth is, it's not entirely clear how we tell whether a maxim can be willed universally – or even how we tell what the maxim of an action is. Kant gave us the promise of a purely rational unifying principle for morality: we have to work out the reality for ourselves.

Kant on the moral law:

'. . . since moral laws ought to hold good for every rational creature, we must derive them from the general concept of a rational being.'

The fundamental resulting law states:

'I am never to act otherwise than so that I could also will that my maxim should become a universal law.' *Fundamental Principles of the Metaphysic of Morals* (1785)

What is the 'maxim' of an action?

If *everyone* worked to free prisoners of conscience, there wouldn't be any prisoners of conscience to set free. If *everyone* worked to cure cancer, there wouldn't be anyone to grow food, and we'd all starve. Does this mean that it's self-defeating (therefore irrational, therefore wrong) to work to free prisoners of conscience or cure cancer?

Cases like these require Kant to specify the maxim of an action rather carefully – and it then becomes doubtful whether there is any universal, purely rational way of saying what the maxim of an action is.

But now, notice that there'd be no point in endorsing this rule, or any other, unless our endorsement produced some effect. Endorsing the rule has to have some bearing on what we do, or at least on what we try to do. So for the notion of endorsing the rule to make any sense, we have to be capable of directing our actions in one way rather than another. We have to be free to set goals for ourselves. Our distinctively human ability to reason entails that we are 'goal-setters'.

So, what about all those possible imitators, whose existence it seems we have to accept if we are to count as rational ourselves? It can plausibly be argued that we have to regard them as goal-setters too, which means that any rational goal-setter (for instance, me) must accept some other (for instance, you) as a rational goal-setter too.

The awkward question now arises whether a purely rational creature could offer any reason for regarding its own goals as more important than the goals of the other goal-setters milling round about. If not, then it follows simply from our nature as rational creatures, that we must accept the goals of others, not indeed as our own, but as equal in importance to our own.

This is a pretty breath-taking conclusion. Is it really true that whenever I impede – or is it just ignore? – the goals of others, I do violence to, or fail to live up to, my true nature as a rational being? In fact, Kant throttles back at this point, and emphasises not so much the particular goals which others may have, as the fact that they do have goals. The new rule which any rational creature has to accept (if Kant is right) says: never treat a human being – even yourself – only as a means to your own ends.

Means and ends

There is an apocryphal story which illustrates the point. Two moral philosophers, one a utilitarian and the other a Kantian, were taken prisoner during World War Two. They agreed that it would maximise happiness – that it was their duty as rational beings – to escape. Unfortunately there was a guard, who would have to be dealt with in some way. The utilitarian argued that the guard, though an enemy, was still a sentient being, whose happiness had to be taken into account. Best therefore to bribe the guard, rather than kill him. The Kantian was horrified. Bribing the guard involves subverting his rationally-chosen goals, and making use of him purely as a means to the prisoners' ends. Far better to kill him. Unable to resolve their moral disagreement, the two remained prisoners for the duration.

In fact, a utilitarian has to be far more willing to sacrifice the individual to the mass than this implies (indeed, this is a standard problem for utilitarianism). Similarly, killing someone might be thought to be the ultimate

Utilitarianism defined (by Jeremy Bentham):

'An action may be said to be conformable to the principle of utility . . . when the tendency it has to augment the happiness of the community is greater than any it has to diminish it.' *Introduction to the Principles of Morals and Legislation* (1789)

Ditto (by John Stuart Mill):

'. . . actions are right in proportion as they tend to promote happiness, wrong as they tend to produce the reverse of happiness. By happiness is intended pleasure, and the absence of pain.' *Utilitarianism* (1861)

Different kinds of utilitarianism

A *positive* utilitarian emphasises the importance of producing pleasure. A *negative* utilitarian thinks it's more important to try to reduce suffering.

An *act*-utilitarian tries to calculate the positive and/or negative consequences for each action individually. A *rule*-utilitarian identifies actions as belonging to a certain type (for example, as theft, or promise-breaking) and judges individual actions according to whether actions of that *type* generally produce happiness and/or reduce suffering.

The most plausible – which is to say, least radical – kind of utilitarianism is negative rule-utilitarianism. However, there's a tendency in all forms of utilitarianism to regard human beings as more or less vehicles for their pleasures or pains. Even if, like Mill, we emphasise that human beings are capable of 'higher' pleasures too, this seems reductive. There is surely more of moral value in a human being than whether he or she is enjoying pleasure or avoiding pain – important as those things are.

in treating them as a means (and Kant's support for capital punishment is therefore a bit problematic). Bribing the guard, it might be argued, merely supports some of his goals at the expense of others. So the story should be taken with a pinch of salt. It does suggest, however, that the application of Kant's rule in real life will often be very debatable.

For example, some moral disapproval of capitalism probably comes from the feeling that buying a worker's labour involves treating him or her as a commodity, a mere means to the employer's ends. Marx sprang from a tradition very strongly influenced by Kant. But suppose the capitalist replies that, on the contrary, the transaction *depends* on the fact that the worker has goals, which he or she will use the money earned to pursue. From this point of view, the capitalist facilitates the worker's goals, and vice versa.

Perhaps it looks, then, as if the transaction itself needn't offend a Kantian (though working conditions etc. might). However, the employer *qua* employer will pay the minimum amount to *anyone* who will do the work for that amount. If robots are cheaper, the employer will use robots. This makes it look as if the employer facilitates the worker's goals more or less accidentally, and to the least degree possible. So we have to ask again: does the capitalist transaction treat workers as merely means to the employer's ends, and so contravene human dignity after all? For a utilitarian like Bentham or Mill, the question can only be whether capitalism produces a greater surplus of happiness over suffering than any available alternative. For Kant, however, this calculus of consequences is precisely *not* the only question. Debate continues.

Kantian morality certainly captures in a systematic way at least *some* of our beliefs about right and wrong, and perhaps that's achievement enough. Kant is also important because he threw light on some 'logical' features of the language we use to make moral judgments – on the fact that moral judgments act like commands, that they are inherently general in their application, that they take precedence over other kinds of recommendation. In the last hundred years, many philosophers have come to think that their professional business is to properly understand these (and other) logical features of moral language, not to tell people what is right and wrong.

Conclusion

Let me end by mentioning a basic problem for Kant, and a way to solve it. I've presented Kant's moral theory as deriving from the view that the distinctive essence of human nature is rationality. But we are obviously creatures of mixed or partial rationality in fact. The problem is: why should we be guided exclusively by the rational part of our nature? What's so good about Reason?

One way forward here is to give up rationality as the essence from which

goal-setting can be derived, and think instead of goal-setting as primary. Suppose that Tomasello is right, and that seeing others as goal-setters is a distinctively human achievement. Suppose too that this 'intentional stance', uniquely achieved by the human infant, is essential, not only for a normal life with other people, but for the kind of cultural learning which makes human society possible. Then if wrong-doing always involves ignoring or trampling on the goals of others (as Kant says), to that extent it involves cutting oneself off from normal social life and inherited culture. The wrong-doer, simply in doing wrong, becomes, to some extent, an outcast. Doing the right thing, by contrast, reinforces everything which is distinctively human in us.

Respecting the goals of others confirms our unique intentional stance, and with it, our place in the social nexus which surrounds us, and in larger human culture. A nice name for this view – if it wasn't already taken – would be 'humanism'.

Notice, finally, what very bad news this is for the attempt to do without final causes. In the first place, 'humanism' clearly makes purposes central to morality. More generally, the very notion of an 'essential human nature', which seems necessary for any secular morality which looks beyond self-interest, probably depends sooner or later on the idea of a final cause. And most generally of all, it seems essential to social life and inherited culture (and so to science too) that we regard others as goal-setters, pursuing purposes or final causes of their own.

Morality and animals

If we derive moral duties from our distinctive human nature, in one way or another, what does that mean for *non*-human animals?

We do not now think animals can be morally good or bad. They have no moral awareness, no moral duties. We might nevertheless have duties towards them, and they might correspondingly have rights against us, even if they could not assert these rights, as it were, in person.

However, if our overriding duty is, as Kant claims, to treat rational beings as ends in themselves, then it looks as if the way we treat *non*-rational beings is not a moral issue (assuming, against Hume and others, that animals cannot reason). If animals are non-rational, then treating an animal well or badly would not be *morally* good or bad. If, on the other hand, we see goal-setting (rather than rationality) as primary, then, since animals are clearly goal-setters, it's easier to see how they would have moral claims on us.

Computers, by contrast, do not set goals for themselves (at least at their present stage of development) and we can therefore treat them as badly as we like.

Do you agree . . . ?

1. **Any action is right as long as its consequences are good.**

   _____

2. **We would not know what is right if God had not told us.**

   _____

3. **The most important thing about human beings is that we see others as goal-setters like ourselves.**

   _____

4. **Capitalism is inherently immoral.**

   _____

CHAPTER 11

Certainty

The last few chapters have explored the consequences, for the concept of action, of rejecting a teleological understanding of causality. We turn in the next few chapters to the consequences for the concept of knowledge, beginning, in the present chapter, with Descartes' attempt to give a new definition of what knowledge is.

So far, we have seen how changes in what we call a 'cause' have led to changes in our picture of scientific method, in our concept of reality, in our understanding (such as it is) of relations between mind and body, and in our image of ourselves as free agents, sometimes saints and often sinners. These same changes in the concept of a cause also have profound implications for our picture of ourselves as rational inquirers, achieving knowledge of the world.

Plato posed an interesting question about knowledge. Suppose you come to a fork in the road. One way leads to Larissa (which is where you want to go) and the other leads somewhere else. What's the difference, Plato asked, between someone who *knows* that it's left for Larissa, and someone who merely believes it and happens to be correct? After all, both of them will get to Larissa.

Another way to ask this question is: what's the difference between knowledge and a lucky guess? Plato thought it had something to do with a kind of stability or fixedness possessed by real knowledge. This was influenced by Parmenides (c.515–440BC), and, along with other things, led Plato into an important dualism of 'What Changes' and 'What Does Not Change'. But we are going to sidestep all that and look instead at Aristotle's answer to the question.

Aristotle on knowledge

Aristotle said that the difference between a belief which happens to be true, and systematic or productive knowledge, lies in this: knowledge which can be made systematic and productive is knowledge of the *cause* of the phenomenon, using the word 'cause' primarily in the sense of final cause (see Chapter 4). I may believe, for example, that every animal which has a heart has kidneys (and let's suppose that this is true). Even if true, it is a mere 'factoid', disconnected and without power. But if I know that the heart exists to pump blood around the body . . . and that blood exists to carry nutrients to, and

The concept of a cause has repercussions for many other ideas:

CAUSE $\left\{\begin{array}{l} \text{SCIENTIFIC METHOD} \\ \text{REALITY} \\ \text{MIND/BODY RELATIONS} \\ \text{FREEDOM} \\ \text{MORALITY} \\ \text{KNOWLEDGE} \ldots \end{array}\right.$

– just one example of the general interconnectedness of problems in philosophy.

Aristotle

waste products from, all parts of the body . . . and if I know that kidneys exist to filter out those waste products . . . *then* I really know something. I understand *why* it is that every animal which has a heart has kidneys. Here we see the problem of defining real or systematic or useful knowledge connect with the problem of causality. As Aristotle says: 'We suppose ourselves to possess unqualified scientific knowledge of a thing . . . when we think that we know the cause on which the fact depends'.

Notice the role of purpose here. Real knowledge depends on knowing what kidneys are *for*, which depends on knowing what blood is *for*, which depends on knowing what the heart is *for*. Remove this sense of purpose or natural function (as Descartes and others did) and Aristotle's distinction between reliable and 'accidental' knowledge collapses. But we still want some distinction of that kind, a distinction between knowledge and a lucky guess. How are we to make this necessary distinction in a world devoid of purpose?

Descartes himself provided what has turned out to be a very influential answer to this question. Real knowledge, according to Descartes, has a solid basis. Like a well-constructed building, it has foundations. And not just any old foundations. Real knowledge has foundations which are *certain*, impossible to doubt. Real knowledge, the scientific edifice, is founded upon solid rock.

Cartesian doubt

How are we to discover these foundations which are impossible to doubt? The most direct method is to doubt everything we possibly can and see what remains, and exactly this is Descartes' famous method of hyperbolical doubt. He applies this method, not because he thinks we do or should doubt everything (in the sense of feel unsure about it), but as a way of identifying things we cannot doubt. This same methodological doubt was also suggested by the scientific revolution (in which Descartes was an important player). The great advances of Copernicus, Kepler and Galileo had involved a willingness to take on the authority of tradition, to question the 'certainties' of received opinion. Descartes thought his method of doubt was merely generalising good scientific procedure, weeding out superstitions.

So what is it possible to doubt? Well, a surprising amount, as it turns out. If you really put your mind to it, you will find it *possible* to doubt that the whole world exists, because the experiences you have which seem to be experiences of the world could all be a dream. Or they could all be provided by an evil demon (or supercomputer, as in *The Matrix*) set on deceiving you. Even that body you think you have could be part of the same grand illusion. In fact, surprising as it seems, *none* of our sense-experiences are beyond all

Copernicus

Kepler

Galileo

possibility of doubt. Then is mathematics certain? No, says Descartes, because of course it's possible to make mistakes, and an evil demon could lead me to make mistakes even in something as simple as 2+3=5.

Fortunately however, Descartes does discover something which it is impossible to doubt. It is impossible to doubt that I think. Let's try to doubt it. Say to yourself, 'I wonder if I am really thinking right now'. And notice that this attempted doubt *is itself a thought*. This means that even the attempt to doubt that I think proves that I do think, which means that it is impossible to doubt that I think. And if I think, I must exist (the famous '*Cogito ergo sum*'). So I exist. But this 'I' which indubitably exists cannot be my body, because my body was disposed of rather early in the method of doubt. So the solid foundation on which real knowledge can be based is this: *I am a non-material thinking thing*.

Working outwards from this narrow basis, Descartes says that if we introspectively examine this indubitable piece of knowledge we will notice a particular clarity and distinctness in it. We see very distinctly what it means and very clearly that it must be true. We feel compelled, in a particular way, to give our assent. Descartes takes this (subjective) clarity and distinctness to be a guarantee of certainty in other cases too, and in this way expands the foundations of knowledge to include such principles as 'Nothing can cause itself', 'A cause must be at least as real as its effect', 'Deceit always comes from weakness', 'God is an infinite spirit' and many more.

Cartesian certainty?

Using these allegedly clear and distinct principles, Descartes now tries to prove, in two separate ways (or it might be three) that God exists. We'll look into proofs of God's existence later. But if God exists and has given me a natural tendency to believe that at least most of my sense-experiences have causes in the world which resemble them, then if this were not true, God would in effect be deceiving me. But since, according to Descartes, deceit always comes from weakness and God is infinitely powerful, it is impossible for God to be a deceiver. So my natural tendency to believe in resembling causes of my sense-experiences must be reliable most of the time, and when it does lead me into error (as when a straight stick looks bent in water for example), the error must be one which, with due care and attention, I can correct. In this way, Descartes re-establishes the general reliability of sense-experience. Our general confidence in the testimony of common sense is justified after all.

Thank goodness for that, you may say. But notice what accompanies the welcome rejection of extravagant Cartesian doubt. First, knowledge is to be

Descartes discovers certainty:

'I observed that, whilst I thus wished to think that all was false, it was absolutely necessary that I, who thus thought, should be something; and as I observed that this truth – I think therefore I am – was so certain that no doubt, however extravagant, could be said by sceptics to be capable of shaking it, I concluded that I might, without scruple, take it as the first principle of the philosophy I was looking for.' *Discourse on Method* (1637)

René Descartes

organised in a hierarchy, with the most certain knowledge at the base and the most provisional, derived from it, at the top. Second, the reconstruction of common sense depends on introspection – it is the clarity and distinctness we find in (some) introspection which guarantees (some) external knowledge as genuine. Third, there is the dualism of matter and mind, which troubles us to this day. I am essentially a non-material thinking thing, though, as is required for one of Descartes' proofs of the existence of God, my mental life is causally continuous with the material world.

This seems a lot to swallow, just to be rid of a doubt which from the beginning was supposed to be purely thought-experimental. And then there is the question: has Descartes really succeeded in banishing hyperbolical doubt? Do the proofs of God's existence work? Are the principles and intuitions which Descartes relies on (as being clear and distinct) really impossible to doubt? Are they even *true*? And what about the very first step – the famous cogito? Does it really follow from the fact that there is a thought, that there must be a thinker? Mightn't there just be thoughts?

Hyperbolical doubt may have been only a methodological device, but if Descartes has raised an evil demon and failed to exorcise it, *we* inherit. What are *we* to say about the possibility of doubt?

Could everything be a dream?

Here's an argument which purports to show that it could not be true that all our experience is a dream.

We learn the meaning of the word 'dream' in the context either of other people's waking testimony of dreams they've had, or of our own experience of surprising discrepancies between dreaming and waking. But if everything is a dream, both these contexts disappear, since both involve waking experience. This implies that, if everything is a dream, the meaning of the word 'dream' must have changed, and we can signal this new meaning – whatever it is – by a new word 'dreem'.

So the sceptical claim is really that everything might be a 'dreem'. Should that worry us? According to the argument, it should not. Dreems are not dreams. We ought to wait until someone explains to us what a 'dreem' is, before we get too concerned.

This argument claims in effect that the dream scenario simultaneously uses and undermines a contrast with waking experience, and so is inconsistent. It can be supplemented by a further argument which tries to show that no concept at all like 'dream' could exist without the contrast with waking.

Arguments along these lines were developed by Norman Malcolm (1911–1990), but somehow it's not easy to state them in a way which is really clear and convincing.

Do you agree . . . ?

1. **We never really know that something is the case until we understand why it is the case.**

_____

2. **Everything we seem to experience could be a dream.**

_____

3. **I think, therefore I exist.**

_____

4. **Knowledge needs a base of absolute certainty.**

_____

CHAPTER 12

The Veil of Appearances

> Descartes used innate ideas to re-build knowledge from the ruins of universal doubt. John Locke based knowledge on experience, and explained sense experience as the appearance to the mind of ideas which *represent* external things. For all its common sense appeal, this view leads, as the present chapter will show, to the very strange view that there are *no* external things.

So, what should we say about the possibility of extravagant, all-inclusive doubt? Well, to be honest, I don't know. Let's see how the situation developed historically.

Descartes' *Meditations* (which I sketched very briefly in the last chapter) appeared in 1641. John Locke lived in France for four years in the 1670s, studying the work of Descartes and Pierre Gassendi (1592–1655), who attacked Descartes' reliance on the clarity and distinctness of ideas as a guarantee of their truth. Locke then spent five years of the turbulent 1680s in Holland, and in 1689, having returned to England, published his *Essay Concerning Human Understanding*.

Descartes himself, as we saw, thought he could overcome the extravagant doubt with which he began and establish knowledge on a firm foundation. Locke, by contrast, argues that we have no innate ideas, destroying in a single empiricist swipe most of Descartes' re-building materials. Locke is also more rigorous than Descartes about the immediate object of knowledge. He says repeatedly that we *directly* know only our own ideas. Anything we know about the world is known indirectly, by means of our ideas: 'knowledge is founded on and employed about our ideas only'. You might think, then, that Locke would be more inclined to Worry about Doubt. But not a bit of it. Like Descartes, Locke is confident that we can prove that God exists. And unlike Descartes, he refuses to take at all seriously the possibility that everything might be a dream.

Locke on knowledge

Locke did think that we ought to be properly modest about what we can know (and he argued from this necessary modesty for toleration about religious belief). Nobody in Locke's time knew the micro-properties of gold, for example, which make it appear yellow. Locke also thought (quite reasonably, given the technology he could imagine at that time) that this knowledge might lie forever beyond our grasp. But he has no doubt that we *can* gain knowledge

John Locke

Nicolas Malebranche: '. . . our mind's immediate object when it sees the sun, for example, is not the sun, but something that is intimately joined to our soul, and this is what I call an *idea*.' *Search After Truth* (1674–75)

Antoine Arnauld (1612–1694) argued against this representative theory of perception that even if the sun itself does not have 'local presence' in the perceiver's head, it can nevertheless have 'objective presence' there (*On True and False Ideas,* 1683).

Descartes himself suggested in a letter that there is 'only so much difference between the soul and its ideas as there is between a piece of wax and the various shapes it can assume.'

about the world, however indirectly. He sees no problem about knowing the world *by way of* knowing our ideas.

And why should he? We can know there is fire in the fireplace indirectly, by way of knowing that there is smoke coming from the chimney, can't we? Yes indeed. But in this case, we can also know that there is fire in the fireplace directly. We can look directly at the fire, or if the door happens to be locked, it is at least possible that someone should get in and look. According to Locke's theory of knowledge, however, no one can *ever* know the world directly. It is in principle impossible for anyone to have direct knowledge of anything beyond their own ideas. Well, how could there be indirect knowledge, if direct knowledge is in principle impossible?

No doubt this also recalls to the alert reader's mind the empiricist principle last mentioned in Chapter 6. If all our concepts come to us from experience (as Locke also asserts) then we cannot have a concept of anything which is in principle beyond our experience. So if the world cannot be directly experienced, it follows that we cannot even have a concept of an external world which causes our ideas. And without the concept we cannot talk intelligibly about such a world. We literally cannot know what we are talking about, if we utter the words 'external world'.

And another thing. Locke says that some of our ideas *resemble* things in the external world. But in order to say that an idea resembles a thing, we have to be able to compare them. On Locke's own account, however, we cannot do this. The best we can manage is to compare one idea with another idea. This fundamental problem in Locke's account is often called the 'veil of appearances', because the subjective appearances of things come down like a veil between us and external things. If we only have (direct) access to our own ideas, how can we possibly get beyond them to the things which supposedly cause them?

Berkeley's Idealism

George Berkeley saw and expressed the 'veil of appearances' problem with great force, and concluded that if we can only know our own ideas, well then, that's all there is. Goodbye, cruel (material) world. Berkeley's theory is called Idealism, for the good and sufficient reason that it says that only ideas exist (well, and spirits too who have them, but you get the idea).

Now you might think that Idealism is a form of scepticism, since it does after all deny the existence of the entire material world. Berkeley himself thought otherwise. He was a religious man (a bishop in fact) and he thought that the non-existence of the material world was a very convenient fact, and not at all in conflict with eternal truth.

Malebranche

Arnauld

Berkeley on the independent existence of matter:

'It is indeed an opinion strangely prevailing amongst men that houses, mountains, rivers, and in a word all sensible objects, have an existence natural or real, distinct from their being perceived by the understanding. But with how great an assurance and acquiescence soever this principle may be entertained in the world, yet whoever shall find in his heart to call it in question, may, if I mistake not, perceive it to involve a manifest contradiction. For what are the forementioned objects but the things we perceive by sense? and what do we perceive besides our own ideas or sensations? and is it not plainly repugnant that any one of these or any combination of them should exist unperceived?' *Principles of Human Knowledge* (1710)

Thus: we have every reason to believe that things continue to exist even when we do not perceive them. The works inside a clock are still there even though no one sees them, and if they weren't, the clock would stop. So things, we think, continue to exist unperceived. But if things are really ideas there's a problem, because an idea cannot exist unperceived (Berkeley believes). That would be an idea which wasn't *anyone's* idea, which is impossible. So if things (that is, ideas) continue to exist when not perceived by us, they must be being perceived by somebody else. And that 'somebody else' is – you guessed it – God. Ideas are independent of *our* perceptions because they are known by God, and the non-existence of matter therefore serves to confirm what faith already held, that God exists. Idealism, far from being a form of scepticism, serves to show (according to Berkeley) how common sense requires belief in God.

Berkeley has at least a couple of other claims to fame. For one thing, he had a new idea about the meaning of the word ' real'. Berkeley argues that to say something exists is to say that it is being perceived (or, as he sometimes says, that it is being or *could be* perceived – a very significant difference, taken up by John Stuart Mill). Berkeley also has some important things to say about classification, which we'll come to in due course.

Conclusion

In the present context, however, the point to emphasise is that Berkeley shot a large hole in Locke's pretensions to common sense. Locke's representative theory of perception (in which mental items represent their external causes) may seem like common sense at first, but it has consequences which are very unpalatable indeed to common sense, because there is no way to show that the mental items really do represent anything at all. As Berkeley says, 'the supposition that things are distinct from Ideas takes away all real truth, & consequently brings in a Universal Scepticism, since all our knowledge is confin'd barely to our own Ideas'. Berkeley himself was personally saved from scepticism by his belief in God. But what if we doubt the existence of God? Why then our name is David Hume, and we have a lot of explaining to do.

George Berkeley

Berkeley's Idealism has been summed up in a pair of well-known limericks:

There was a young man who said, 'God,
I find it exceedingly odd
That this tree I see
Should continue to be,
When there's no one about in the Quad.'

'Dear Sir, Your astonishment's odd:
I am always about in the Quad,
And that's why the tree
Will continue to be,
Since observed by Yours Faithfully, God.'

Do you agree . . . ?

1. **Human beings have the ability to form mental images.**

   _____

2. **When a person looks at the sun, an image of the sun appears in his or her mind.**

   _____

3. **Mental images, including those derived from perception, can resemble real things.**

   _____

4. **In order to be able to say that A resembles B, we must be able to compare A and B.**

   _____

CHAPTER 13

Scepticism

In Chapter 2 we looked at Hume's argument to show that it is not reasonable to believe that the future will resemble the past. We now consider another example of a belief dismissed by Hume as unreasonable – belief in a continuing self.

We have been tracing the gradual erosion of Descartes' confidence that most of our common sense beliefs could be rationally justified. The complete collapse of this confidence was postponed in Locke by failure to see the seriousness of the 'veil of appearances' problem, and in Berkeley by belief in God. The exact nature of Hume's religious views is controversial, but he was certainly suspected of atheism in his own time, and lost at least two jobs because of it. Whatever his personal beliefs in the matter, it is clear that he does not want to make anything in his philosophical system depend on belief in God. The result is unmitigated scepticism, and my next task is to explain how Hume, and in the two chapters following this how Kant and Reid, responded to the demonstration that most of our deepest claims to knowledge are at best irrational, and at worst nonsensical.

Hume wrote his *Treatise of Human Nature* in his twenties. It is a complex, sophisticated, ironical work, and much ink has been spilled in attempts to interpret, and refute, it. What follows is the merest sketch.

Reason and imagination

Hume's recurrent strategy is to take some deep-seated belief (such as the belief that the future will resemble the past) and argue that it is impossible to defend the belief by reason. We hold the belief, not because we have good reasons for doing so, but through the action of the imagination, by a kind of conditioned reflex or mental automatism (see Chapter 2). There are two steps here: first, a demonstration that attempts to rationally justify a given belief are doomed, and second, an explanation of how the belief in question is actually produced in us. It is not and could not be produced by reason: how then do we come to hold it? What psychological mechanism produces it? The first step casts Hume in the role of master sceptic for modern times. The second casts him in the role of founder of psychology.

If either of these steps is correct, it seems to follow that it is not reasonable to believe the things we all do believe. We cannot rationally justify our most fundamental beliefs. But Hume takes two attitudes to this. On the one hand, he takes mischievous pleasure in demonstrating the 'fallaciousness and

Hume on scepticism:

Philosophical scepticism, according to Hume, reveals 'the whimsical condition of mankind, who must act and reason and believe – though they are not able, by their most diligent enquiry, to satisfy themselves concerning the foundation of these operations, or to remove the objections which may be raised against them.' *Enquiry* (1748)

Scepticism comes in various guises, and it has been put to many different uses. Fundamentally, scepticism means doubting or questioning things we normally take for granted. *Humean* scepticism doubts or questions, not the truth of these things, but the reasonableness of believing them.

The following motion was put to the General Assembly of the Church of Scotland in 1756:

'. . . there is one person styling himself David Hume, Esq. who hath arrived at such a degree of boldness as publicly to avow himself the author of books containing the most rude and open attacks upon the glorious gospel of Christ . . . therefore the Assembly [should] appoint . . . a committee . . . to call him before them . . .'

The General Assembly, to its eternal credit, threw this motion out by fifty votes to seventeen.

imbecility' of Reason, so highly vaunted in the Enlightenment. It was this which led Russell to blame Hume for ushering in the irrationalities of Romanticism. But on the other hand, Hume often presents Nature (which produces these important beliefs in us and thus compensates for the impotence of Reason) as stronger and more trustworthy than Reason. He *endorses* the unreasoned beliefs produced in us by Nature, by the 'permanent, irresistible and universal' working of the imagination. The end result is something like this: we have to accept that we are unreasonable creatures – and be glad! Better self-deceived than dead.

Let me give you a (not entirely representative) example. Descartes had argued, as we saw, that the existence of a thought proves the existence of a thing which thinks. Hume carefully takes this 'thinking thing' apart, and finds it to be – a mirage.

Hume on the self

The empiricist principle 'no concepts except through experience' comes into play once again. Hume asks: do we ever experience this thinking thing? When we introspect do we ever stumble across a Self? No we don't, he says. And couldn't either, because anything we experience would be an *object* of experience, not the *subject* which is supposed to have them. But if we have no experience and hence no concept of a Self, we can't even understand what a Self is supposed to be. And in this case, it's plainly impossible to rationally arrive at the existence of the 'thinking thing'. Descartes' reconstruction therefore falls at the first hurdle. End of step one.

It's natural to inquire now why we find ourselves believing that there *is* an enduring Self, a subject of experience (here beginneth step two). Since we don't, according to Hume, have any concept of a Self, we can't really believe that one exists. Rather, we must be wrongly expressing some other belief in those (strictly meaningless) terms. This other belief, Hume claims, is the belief that 'something' unites all the experiences we have into a single group or bundle. The connectedness of one experience with the next sets the natural inertia of the imagination in motion, and we find ourselves irresistibly inclined to believe that *all* our experiences are connected into a single whole. Unfortunately, as Hume shows, there's no very appealing candidate for this unifying 'something'. It can't be content, because we have all sorts of very variegated experiences. It can't be experienced continuity, because there are breaks in the stream of experience. It can't be dependence on the same body, because our experiences of this 'same body' are just others among the flow of experiences we are trying to unify. The imagination therefore supplies a unifying something, a Self, though on analysis we can see that what it supplies is a 'fiction' if not outright nonsense.

Russell wrote:

'It was inevitable that such a self-refutation of rationality should be followed by a great outburst of irrational faith ... The growth of unreason throughout the nineteenth century and what has passed of the twentieth is a natural sequel to Hume's destruction of empiricism.' *History of Western Philosophy* (1945)

Empiricism: 1
Self: 0

'It must be some one impression that gives rise to every real idea. But self or person is not any one impression, but that to which our several impressions and ideas are supposed to have a reference. If any impression gives rise to the idea of self, that impression must continue invariably the same, through the whole course of our lives, since self is supposed to exist after that manner. But there is no impression constant and invariable. Pain and pleasure, grief and joy, passions and sensations succeed each other, and never all exist at the same time. It cannot, therefore, be from any of these impressions, or from any other, that the idea of self is derived; and consequently there is no such idea.' *Treatise* (1739)

Hume on the imagined self:

'In order to justify to ourselves this absurdity [the absurdity of regarding the stream of disconnected experiences as a single unified whole], we ... feign some new and unintelligible principle, that connects the objects together, and prevents their interruption or variation.' *Treatise* (1739)

This example is untypical (though conveniently relevant to Descartes) because Hume cannot in this case endorse the belief we naturally arrive at. His empiricist conviction that concepts must derive from prior experience implies, more irresistibly in this case than elsewhere, that the belief in an enduring Self is strictly nonsensical. So he suggests that in this case, the natural processes of belief formation have run away with themselves: in fact, there's no need for a single unifying something since we have no clear or definite idea of the unity of a bundle of experiences.

But this really opens the proverbial can of worms. In the first place, it is beginning to emerge that if we endorse the natural, causal processes of belief formation, we must concede that Nature can produce concepts where there has been no experience. What we naturally believe is that there is an enduring Self *in addition to* the stream of experiences. This clearly conflicts with the empiricist insistence that all our concepts come from *within* the stream of experience. In the second place, suggesting that the natural processes of belief formation have gone too far in this case implies that there is some higher court of appeal. Nature trumps Reason, but now it seems that something can trump Nature. Well, what could it be?

In a famous Appendix to the *Treatise*, Hume says frankly that he is not happy with his account of our belief in an enduring Self. It's notoriously difficult to work out from what he says there what he takes the problem to be. But if the underlying problem is that even Nature cannot produce concepts out of thin air, then either the empiricist thesis that all our concepts are derived from experience has to be rejected, or it becomes impossible to endorse our natural common sense beliefs. It's one thing to endorse a belief you cannot justify with reasons, but to endorse something you can't understand is absurd.

So far we have been looking at the complicated scepticism of Hume's youthful masterpiece, the *Treatise of Human Nature*. But Hume also wrote a number of important essays – on miracles, on aesthetics and economics, on suicide, on the immortality of the soul – and though some of these were too incendiary to be published in his lifetime, others emerged to seal his reputation as a dangerous free-thinker. In his essay 'On Miracles', for example, he proves by apparently cast-iron logic that it can never be reasonable to accept on the testimony of others that a miracle has occurred. Since the whole of modern Christian belief is founded on accepting the testimony of the gospels concerning miracles, this was a sufficiently alarming proposition.

Hume on miracles

Here's the argument. Hume first of all defines a miracle as 'a transgression of a law of nature by a particular volition of the Deity, or by the interposition of

David Hume

some invisible agent'. He further defines a reasonable person as one who proportions his or her belief to the evidence: more evidence produces stronger belief, less evidence produces doubt. Now that it's clear what we're talking about, let's compare the amount of evidence we have for a law of nature, on one hand, with the amount of evidence we have for the reliability of testimony, on the other. It quickly becomes obvious that we have more evidence for a law of nature than for any other factual belief. *All* our experience supports a law of nature – that's why it's a law. By contrast, we know perfectly well that human testimony is subject to all kinds of problems. There are honest misunderstandings and mistakes, there are more or less deliberate omissions and embellishments, and there is the whole gamut of mendacity, from harmless fibs to outright whopping lies. This means that the evidence for a law of nature is always 100 per cent: the evidence for human testimony is always considerably less. A reasonable person, therefore, will always believe more strongly in the law than in any report that it has been transgressed. Which is to say that a reasonable person will never believe testimony for a miracle.

Well, this is an interesting argument, and if there's something wrong with it, we haven't yet reached a consensus on what it is. In the second half of the essay, Hume concedes that there *are* cases in which it would be reasonable to believe – or at least investigate – reports of some unprecedented happening. But only, he argues, if the reports were exceptionally uniform and well-attested, and only if the event in question was of no advantage to the 'witnesses'. Since the reports of Christian and other miracles fall far below these requirements, the sceptical conclusion – that it can never be reasonable to believe reports of a miracle – must stand. Many of his devout contemporaries felt, understandably, that after reading Hume, the believer could 'plunge no deeper into the abyss of scepticism, and encounter no antagonist more acute or insinuating'.

Conclusion

Apart from his important contributions to the process of secularisation, Hume gave a sharp and systematic demonstration of the fact that our basic common sense beliefs (in causal necessity and regularity, in an enduring Self, in an external world) do *not* have rational foundations, and turned attention instead to the psychological mechanisms which compel us to accept them. He had a rare ability, or compulsion – which inspired Einstein among others – to pursue a line of thought to the bitter end, no matter how difficult or threatening the terrain.

The essay 'On Miracles' ends with a wonderful example of Hume's poised – and in this case poisoned – irony:

'. . . upon the whole, we may conclude, that the *Christian religion* not only was at first attended with miracles, but even at this day cannot be believed by any reasonable person without one. Mere reason is insufficient to convince us of its veracity: And whoever is moved by *Faith* to assent to it, is conscious of a continued miracle in his own person, which subverts all the principles of his understanding, and gives him a determination to believe what is most contrary to custom and experience.'

Einstein wrote (in his *Autobiographical Notes*):

'The type of critical thinking required for the discovery of [relativity] was decisively furthered, in my case, especially by the reading of David Hume's and Ernst Mach's philosophical writings.'

Do you agree . . . ?

1. **Every human being has an enduring self or subject of experience.**

2. **We never encounter this enduring self in introspection.**

3. **All our concepts are derived from experience.**

4. **The processes by which we come to hold our basic beliefs are rational processes.**

5. **It can never be rational to believe reports of a miracle.**

CHAPTER 14

Transcendental Confidence

Rejecting the Aristotelian definition because of its dependence on causes-as-purposes, and substituting a definition of knowledge as whatever survives methodological doubt, seems to lead inevitably to scepticism. In this chapter we examine Kant's attempt to reinstate informative innate ideas as a way of combating Hume's scepticism.

Pursuing Cartesian knowledge to the bitter end, then, seems to leave us with very little of it. In his various 'step one' arguments, Hume demolishes all claims to get beyond the pale of our experiences in any reasonable way. Before the eighteenth century was out, however, there were two responses to this crisis, which tried to shore up the foundations of knowledge. One (due to Immanuel Kant) had its greatest influence in the nineteenth century. The other (due to Thomas Reid) has been more influential in the twentieth.

Kant claimed to have brought about a 'Copernican revolution' in philosophy, and this self-confident metaphor seems to work in at least two ways. Copernicus reversed relations between the earth and the sun, placing the sun at the centre. This meant that much of what we see – the sun appearing to rise and set for example – is in fact due to the motion of the earth. We have to make allowances for our own limited and misleading point of view. In the same way, many of the most basic elements of experience, according to Kant, are contributed by us, aspects of our cognitive point of view, not true of the world 'out there'. Secondly, Kant reverses relations between immediate experience and common-sense belief. Descartes and Locke may have seen immediate experience as infallible, as the solid earth we stand on, and common-sense belief as dependent, as the sun we have to reach for. But Hume, Kant thought, had shown that on this model, it is impossible to reach the sun. We cannot rationally infer from immediate experience to common-sense belief. According to Kant, therefore, our fundamental common-sense beliefs come first. We have them *before* we have any experiences, and we contribute them to the raw sensory input we receive, in order to make intelligible experiences possible: our common-sense beliefs 'are not derived from experience, but experience is derived from them'.

Kant on innate ideas

Now it would not be at all plausible to say that babies are born believing, for example, that the sky is blue. Nor does believing that the sky is blue seem

Immanuel Kant

Kant on things in themselves:

'Essences of the understanding [that is, noumena or things in themselves] are hereby admitted only by the emphasising of this rule, which admits of no exception, that we know nothing definite whatever of these pure essences of the understanding, neither can we know anything of them ...'
Prolegomena (1783)

necessary in order for us to make sense of our experience. So Kant's defence does not apply to particular common-sense beliefs, or even to quite general ones. Kant's aim is to defend only the most fundamental elements of common sense – belief in causal relations, in human freedom, in Euclidean geometry and Newtonian physics, in a subject of experience, in God. Belief in an external world Kant defends in a highly qualified way. There must be *something* out there, he thinks, but we can't say anything at all about what it's like. Or to be precise, we can't say anything about what it's really like, in itself (that is, about what Kant calls 'noumena'). We can of course say plenty about how it seems to us (that is, about 'phenomena').

So Kant defends the most fundamental elements of common sense as essential pre-conditions for making sense of our experience. What does that mean exactly? I wonder if you remember Descartes' distinction between factitious, adventitious and innate ideas? As a good empiricist, Hume follows Locke in rejecting the third category, and this leads, as I said at the end of the last chapter, to the perplexing conclusion that we do not in fact possess certain ideas we think we do possess. The idea of a continuing Self for example, is not derived from experience (not adventitious) and can be constructed (i.e. can be factitious) only if we 'feign' some 'unintelligible' principle. So if, as empiricism claims, the idea is not innate, it follows (paradoxically) that we do not in fact possess any idea of an enduring Self. Kant responds by reinstating the third category. The most fundamental elements of common sense appear in us, not from any constructive effort of our own (reasoned or imaginative), and not from experience. They are *a priori* (prior to all experience). And in spite of this, they carry genuine information about the world (of appearances) – they are *synthetic*. In short, we have substantive innate ideas.

And yet the word 'substantive' could mislead, because these innate elements are more like categories or organising principles than ordinary judgments or beliefs. They provide a framework into which our day-to-day experiences can fit. Without this framework our experiences would be unintelligible – a riot of colours, a medley of noises, a shambles of smells and tastes and feels. This would never do of course, and so we have categories, organising principles, framework concepts. What we might represent as a belief that every event has a cause, for example, is really a heuristic for bringing otherwise bewildering experiences together as cause and effect. What we might represent as a belief in an omnipotent and merciful creator, is really 'a *regulative principle* of reason, which directs us to look upon all connection in the world *as if* it originated from an all-sufficient necessary cause'. In short, certain frameworks or regulative principles are necessary for us to make sense out of our experience. Kant says frameworks and principles which are necessary in this way are 'transcendentally' necessary.

Belief and experience

We're familiar with beliefs which come from experience. You know the weight of this book, for example, because you've picked it up. This kind of knowledge is called – in a rather unhelpful piece of jargon – *a posteriori*. It's posterior, or subsequent, to experience. Knowledge which doesn't come from experience (if there is any) is called *a priori*. Maths and logic are the usual suspects.

The same distinction between *a priori* and *a posteriori* can also be applied to concepts, the building blocks of knowledge. An empiricist holds that all our concepts are *a posteriori*: Kant claims that the most basic ones are *a priori*. But because Kant also says these *a priori* concepts are – in another bad bit of jargon – *synthetic* or informative, they must be rather like knowledge. They carry information. In this way, Kant demands from us greater clarity about the distinction – which we tend to take for granted – between concepts and beliefs.

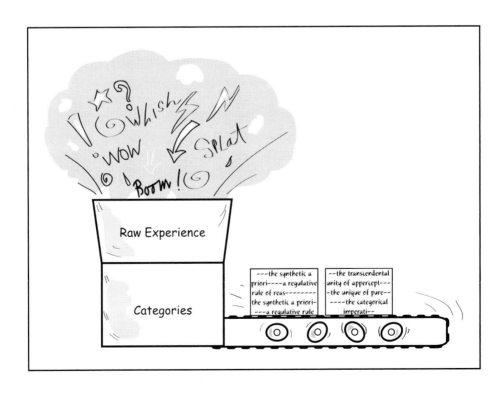

A transcendental self

Kant argues in response to Hume, for example, that the notion of a self is transcendentally necessary. Let me begin by quoting Kant:

> 'that I think' must be able to accompany all my representations; for, if not, something that could not be thought at all would be represented in me, which means just as well as that the representation would be either impossible or at least nothing for me. (*Critique of Pure Reason*, 1781)

What is this 'something that could not be thought'? Is it a representation unaccompanied by 'that I think'? Well, it is of course psychologically possible to become so absorbed in the content of a representation that we lose our sense of who we are or what we're doing. We become, as we say, *lost* in admiration of a colour, for example. So perhaps Kant really means (by this 'something that could not be thought') a representation accompanied by 'that I do not think'. This new, composite representation would at least seem to be impossible. But does the impossibility of adding 'that I do not think' imply that it must always be possible to add 'that I think'? Not if, as Hume has been arguing, they are both empty verbiage (since the 'I' is supposed to be something outside experience). On this interpretation, in other words, Kant's impossible representation just assumes that this element 'I' is available, which is not to argue against Hume but simply to take for granted what Hume denies.

So let's go back to our first guess, and suppose that Kant means a representation unaccompanied by 'that I think'. Why can't this be thought? Why is it impossible? Kant's argument *might* be that the only way to synthesise different representations into enduring external objects (so as to make sense of them) is to regard them as belonging to the same subject, the same 'I'. Any representation without this common element of 'that I think' would be isolated from all other representations, Kant might be claiming, and therefore unintelligible.

Hume, however, has a detailed account of how the imagination unifies impressions into objects, without relying (at least overtly) on their being received by the same subject of experience, and a very similar account was advanced by A. J. Ayer (1910–1989) thirty years ago. It's also difficult to see what unifying function the Kantian 'I' could really have, given that it's 'the mere form of consciousness', an unknowable noumenon about which nothing can be said.

But let's not get too involved in the details. Some languages demand a first-person pronoun: '*I* think such-and-such', '*I* see yonder what-not', '*I*'m going to

Kant on the unknowable nature of noumena:

'What objects may be in themselves, and apart from all this receptivity of our sensibility, remains completely unknown to us.' *Critique of Pure Reason* (1781)

The transcendental necessity of causality:

'Experience itself – in other words, empirical knowledge of appearances – is thus possible only in so far as we subject the succession of appearances, and therefore all alteration, to the law of causality; and, as likewise follows, the appearances, as objects of experience, are themselves possible only in conformity with the law.' *Critique of Pure Reason* (1781)

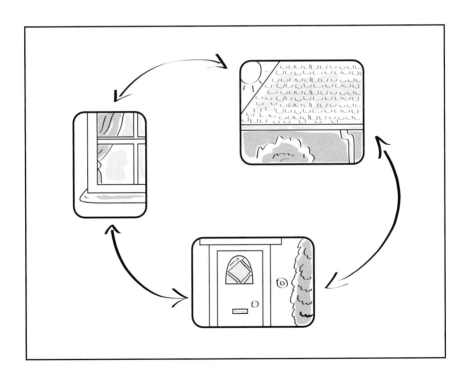

do it'. Others don't. The question is: what does this 'I' come to? What can it possibly be? Might it be like the 'it' of 'It's raining'? Even if 'that I think' does indeed have to accompany all our representations, or be available to accompany them, the question still remains: what does this word 'I' *mean*?

Transcendental causes

Here's another example of a transcendental argument (based, that is, on our need for frameworks to organise experience), this time directed against Hume's account of causality. Kant points out that we distinguish between a sequence of experiences which is in the order it is because of some subjective factor (for example, because I look this way, then that), and a sequence which is objectively ordered. Suppose we couldn't make this distinction. Then, Kant argues, we couldn't attribute the order of our experiences to anything outside ourselves: 'We should then have only a play of representations, relating to no object'. And in this case, it would be impossible for us to achieve experience in the normal sense of the term, experience of the world. So what do we need to make the distinction between subjective and objective ordering? Kant's argument is that we need the idea of cause and effect. It's because A causes B and B causes C (in the case of objective ordering) that we always experience them in the order A, then B, then C. So the idea of cause and effect is a precondition of making sense of any stretch of experience, not (as empiricists like Hume supposed) something which we derive from raw experience.

This is just a sketch of Kant's argument, of course. Once we begin to look into some of the links in this argument, things get very murky indeed. But let's concentrate on the main question: is it really impossible to construct out of disconnected experiences a distinction between subjective and objective ordering?

Suppose we always have experiences A, B and C in that order, whereas we have experiences X, Y and Z in any old order. Then A is always followed by B, whereas X is not always followed by Y, or by Z. On Hume's account, constant conjunction prompts the imagination to expect B given A, and so to generate the idea of a connection between A and B. Accordingly, we regard A and B as causally connected and X and Y as 'loose and disconnected' (from each other at least). What's more, my looking this way or that (L1 and L2, let's call them) are also experienced. If I find a constant conjunction between X and L1, and between Y and L2, then I come to believe in causal relations here too. In this way I can distinguish between an order L1 – X – L2 – Y which depends on events which I can will to occur (L1 and L2) and an order A – B – C which does not. Isn't this the distinction Kant thought Hume could not generate, between subjective and objective ordering? And isn't Hume's account superior

Watching a boat sail downstream, the events we observe follow a fixed order: first it passes the windmill, then the forest, then the castle. When we look at the different parts of a house, by contrast, we find no unchanging order in our experiences. We might look first at the roof, then at an upper floor window, then at the front door – or we might look at the same parts of the house in some other order instead.

Thus, some sequences of experience have an objective order, and others have at most a subjective order. Kant's claim is that this distinction does not generate but presupposes the idea of causality. It cannot *generate* the idea of causality because that idea is already needed even to make sense of a sequence of experience, as experience of a house or boat.

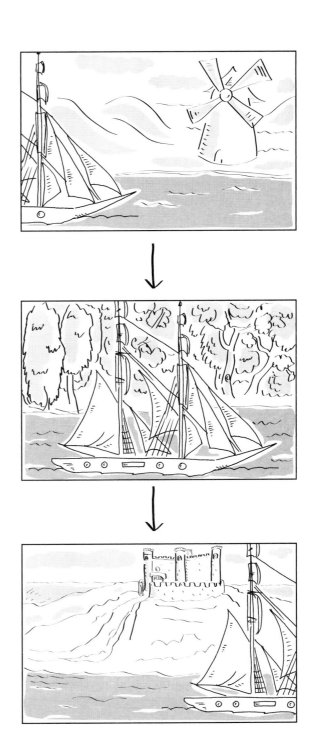

– or at least more unified – in bringing causal relations into the subjective sequences too?

Finally, even if we grant that the distinction (between subjective and objective order) can only be made by ascribing causal relations in the one case and not the other, the question still remains: what does it *mean* to say that A causes B? We looked at Hume's striking and prophetic answer in Chapter 2 (it means that A-like things are constantly conjoined with B-like things). As in the case of the self, however, Kant gives the question up as unanswerable (though continuing to use the concept in a fundamental way).

Conclusion

Whatever we think of particular transcendental arguments, or even of transcendental arguments in general, Kant certainly introduces some important new ideas. Are our 'fundamental beliefs' really 'regulative principles'? Are they innate? Is there a noumenal world forever beyond anything we might experience? Kant's tremendous obscurity has also, strangely, added to his appeal. Hacking one's way through thickets of jargon, one *does* have the feeling, from time to time, of breaking through to glimpse some exhilarating vista, some profound discovery – before the jungle closes in again.

The Kantian idea I find most interesting, for the problem of scepticism, is this: if the fundamentals of common sense are not beliefs but organising principles, then justifying them should not be a matter of bringing forward sufficient evidence, but of showing that they succeed in organising well. And if their success consists in making experience intelligible, then perhaps the indubitable fact that our experience *is* intelligible to us is enough to show that the fundamentals of common sense are justified. If so, we would have finally succeeded in exorcising the demon of Cartesian doubt. Wouldn't that be nice, after everything we've been through?

Beliefs, rules and attitudes

What is the difference between a belief and an 'organising principle'? The obvious answer is that a belief can be true or false: an organising principle is something like a rule. 'Put the heavy things at the bottom of your shopping bag' isn't true or false. It's a rule which helps avoid disaster.

So for example, if 'There are other minds' is a *belief,* then I ought to have some evidence for it. But even if I can drum up some sort of evidence, it isn't my actual reason for believing that other people have minds, and it doesn't justify the unconditional way I believe. Perhaps, then, 'There are other minds' is misleadingly expressed. Perhaps it would be better to phrase it as a rule, saying 'Interpret others' actions as if they had minds'.

Unfortunately, this still prompts the question, 'OK, but do they *really* have minds?' If the aim is to outflank this question, a more radical rephrasing is required, which gets away – somehow – from the idea that minds or experiences are items which either exist or don't exist. It *might* be possible to see 'There are other minds' as not asserting a fact at all, for example, but as expressing an attitude or cluster of emotions.

Do you agree . . . ?

1. **All information about the world comes to us through experience.**

   _____

2. **Belief in God is really a regulative principle of reason.**

   _____

3. **We could not make sense of experience without ascribing it to a continuing self.**

   _____

4. **It is impossible to construct the idea of a causal relationship from our raw sensory exerience.**

   _____

CHAPTER 15

Common Sense

Hume's scepticism is of course in stark opposition to common sense, and in this chapter we look first at Thomas Reid's attempt to identify the basic mistake of Descartes, Locke and Hume, and then at his reassertion of the authority of common sense.

Thomas Reid, like Kant, thought it was necessary to go back to an error of Descartes in order to refute Hume. Not the error of taking ideas as foundations for beliefs – the more fundamental error of having anything to do with ideas at all. Kant distinguishes things as they seem to us from things as they are in themselves, phenomena from noumena. To someone like Reid, unknowable things-in-themselves are still too sceptical by half.

Reid makes a sweeping attack on the picture of ideas as discrete, identifiable particulars. Ideas are not to be seen as the mental analogues of *things*. They are the mental analogues of *acts*. Not items – actions.

Descartes, and more clearly Locke, thought that an idea is a thing, a kind of inner object which the observer can inspect. But then as we have seen, the 'veil of appearances' problems seem to lead inevitably to scepticism. Another problem is that the Lockean model of perception also threatens a regress of ever more shadowy ideas. If inspecting, examining, observing a tree is understood as awareness of a tree-resembling mental object, then shouldn't awareness of this new mental object be understood in the same way, as involving a further mental object which resembles the first one, leading to a regress? Or if, on the other hand, we can be aware of ideas without a mental intermediary, why can we not see a tree in the same direct way? According to Reid, seeing a tree is of course mediated by lots of physical processes, but it is *not* also mediated by a mental entity.

Reid on ideas

For Reid then, ideas are *modifications*, not objects, of consciousness. He writes,

> ... if by ideas are meant only the acts or operations of our minds in perceiving, remembering or imagining objects, I am far from calling in question the existence of those acts ... The ideas of whose existence I require the proof, are not operations of any mind, but supposed objects of those operations. (*Essays on the Intellectual Powers of Man*, 1785)

your most obedient servant

Tho. Reid

Thomas Reid (1710–1796)

Reid studied at Marischal College in Aberdeen and became librarian there, pursuing his interests in mathematics (a family tradition on his mother's side). In his late twenties, he followed the family tradition on his father's side and became a minister. The publication of Hume's *Treatise* at this time was a transforming event in Reid's life.

In 1752 he became professor of philosophy at Kings College in Aberdeen, and in 1764 he succeeded Adam Smith as professor of moral philosophy at Glasgow.

As a person he seems to have been modest and peaceable – happy to live in the world of ideas.

The *objects* of consciousness, according to Reid, are the things we are conscious of – the real Eiffel Tower, for example, not a mental image or other mental representation of it. For Reid, the mind does perceive, but what it perceives (in all normal cases) is the external thing.

Does this help? Well, given that the Eiffel Tower when I see it does 'get into my mind' somehow, how does it do it? There doesn't appear to be room for the real Eiffel Tower in there, but there must be room for a mental image of it. (There's a neat argument in Augustine, by the way, which supports the same kind of move. When I talk about forgetfulness, Augustine says, if I had the real thing in mind, I'd forget what I was talking about. So I must operate with a *representation* of forgetfulness, which is what gives meaning to the word.)

But if the real thing isn't 'in my mind', it seems that Reid must either try to explain how the mind makes perception possible (that is, must propose an operations-only account to rival Locke's representational-items theory) or else in some way resist the demand for a mind-based explanation. The second alternative has been developed in the twentieth century by Ludwig Wittgenstein (1889–1951), and I'm not going to say any more about it here. The first alternative looks fraught with peril. If there isn't a representational 'thing', is there a representational 'activity'? To involve no mental objects, this representational activity would (it seems) have to be something like a mime, without props, and without even a body. It's hard enough to make sense of that, but in any case the claim that the mind's activity is representational seems enough to generate the familiar veil of appearances problems. How could we possibly confirm that a given stretch of mental activity represents, for example, the Eiffel Tower?

Reid on 'suggestion'

But there are other resources in Reid's position. He claims that a stretch of mental activity prompts us to think about the real object, not by resembling it, but in the way that a word prompts us to think about the thing it stands for. The written or spoken word 'sun' does not at all resemble the thing it stands for, yet the one 'suggests' or leads us to think of the other. In some similar way, the mind's activity when we perceive makes us think of the external thing, and believe in its existence, without resembling it.

Here again the two alternatives arise: is this really an attempt to explain how the mind makes perception possible, or is it a way of rejecting the demand for any such explanation? When Reid says that a sensation creates a concept of the external object and produces a belief in its existence 'by a natural kind of magic' or 'by a simple and . . . inexplicable act of the mind' it looks as if he might be rejecting the demand for a mentalistic explanation,

A mental representation of the
Eiffel Tower . . . or . . .

. . . a stream of mental operations?

Language, thought and reality (according to Reid)

saying in effect that acts or objects of the mind cannot *explain* perception. On this view, however, the idea of 'suggestion' indicates just a brute tendency to believe, which Hume will be happy to concede. *Of course* we naturally develop certain concepts and beliefs under the impact of experience. Hume's question is: are those processes of development governed by reason or the imagination?

If, on the other hand, the analogy with language is supposed to *explain* how our beliefs about the external world arise, then even though no claims about resemblance are involved, problems similar to the veil of appearances problems still arise. We can associate the word 'sun' with the real sun because we have independent access to both word and thing. If we are supposed to take Reid's analogy seriously, there must also be a learned association between stretches of perceiving-type mental activity and external objects. But any learned association between the mental and the external requires a non-mental way of getting access to the external. Otherwise it's just an association between different stretches of mental activity and, once again, idealism looms. Unfortunately, if the mental has been seized on to explain what makes perception possible – if we insist on a mentalistic explanation – there cannot be any non-mental way of getting this access.

The authority of common sense

Let's turn then to another anti-sceptical line, Reid's stress on the authority of common sense. Reid offers three marks of a self-evident belief:

1. the belief is universal. Reid writes, 'a consent of ages and nations, of the learned and the vulgar, ought, at least, to have great authority, unless we can show some prejudice, as universal as that consent is, which might be the cause of it.' Reid here tries to throw the burden of proof onto the sceptic: it is not up to common sense to justify itself, rather, it is up to the sceptic to demonstrate 'some prejudice'. Unfortunately, demonstrating prejudices (specifically, the inertia of the imagination) was just what Hume went in for.

2. the belief appears in the mind early enough to guarantee that it is 'not the effect of education or false reasoning'.

3. the belief is 'so necessary in the conduct of life that a man cannot live and act according to the rules of common prudence without [it]'. A belief in the external world, or in reliable causal relations, seems essential if we are to negotiate our surroundings successfully.

A belief with these three features, Reid claims, does not need to be justified. It is, as it were, innocent until proven guilty. What's more, since justification involves supporting something we are less confident of by means of something we are more confident of, and since there is *nothing* we are more confident of than the beliefs Hume attacked, justification of these

Reid on the authority of common sense:

'To what purpose is it for philosophy to decide against common sense in this or any other matter? The belief in a material world is older, and of more authority, than any principles of philosophy. It declines the tribunal of reason, and laughs at all the artillery of the logician.' *An Inquiry into the Human Mind* (1764)

Reid on self-evident truth:

'Evidence is the sole and ultimate ground of belief, and self-evidence is the strongest possible ground of belief; and he who desires reason for believing what is self-evident knows not what he means.' (unpublished manuscript)

Hume writes:

'We may well ask, *What causes induce us to believe in the existence of body?* but 'tis in vain to ask, *Whether there be body or not?* That is a point which we must take for granted in all our reasonings.' *Treatise* (1739)

In other cases (for example in his discussion of the Self), Hume does ask both questions. But the first question is the fundamental one for him.

fundamental beliefs is, in the nature of things, impossible. The sceptic, in demanding a proof or justification, is demanding the impossible (which is of course unreasonable). Scepticism can therefore be dismissed as irrational.

Hume, however, does not demand a proof or a justification (or so it seems to me). His question is simply: where does this belief come from? How *do* we arrive at our belief, for example, that the future will resemble the past? His answer, in case after fundamental case, is that the belief is produced not by reasoning, but by a blind psychological mechanism.

On the other hand, Hume does tend to assume that a belief which is not produced by reasoning is not a reasonable belief. And it might be possible to argue, against this assumption of Hume's, that a belief with Reid's three marks of self-evidence can reasonably be held, even without reasons for holding it. But since Hume was perfectly clear that it is inevitable and *good* that we believe these things, there is some danger of this deteriorating into a semantic debate about the tag 'reasonable', with all Hume's substantive points conceded. Reid says, for example, '. . . we agree with the author of the "Treatise of Human Nature", in this, that our belief in the continuance of nature's laws is not derived from reason. It is an instinctive prescience . . . without [which] we should be incapable of receiving the information of nature by means of experience.'

Conclusion

The last part of this remark brings out a similarity between Reid and Kant (since it defends our fundamental common sense beliefs as springing from our own nature and as necessary for any experience). But where Kant's response to Hume was adventurous and creative, Reid's overall response – apart from his claim that 'common sense' can create concepts and authorise beliefs – is critical and in a sense negative. He argues that there are no discrete, identifiable, mental entities intervening between the knowing mind and the object of its knowledge. There is nothing indirect (in Locke's sense) about our knowledge of the world. There is no burden of proof for common sense. The rationality of a belief is not always a matter of having reasons for believing it. *Perhaps* he is moving towards the view that there is no need for, or no possibility of, a mentalistic explanation of perception. This negative quality might make Reid less of a thrill to read than Kant (though he is far easier stylistically), but in essence it should be an advantage. If Reid's negative points can rescue us from Humean scepticism, we will have risked less in the process.

Transcendental Idealism and Common Sense

Both Kant and Reid were the originators of 'schools'. Kant was seized upon by a line of Romantics – Fichte, Schelling, Hegel – who thought he was saying that we can only understand art, morality and the world by looking deeply into our selves.

Reid's followers – Beattie, Oswald, Stewart – toed the party line more closely, and tended to represent a rather conservative reaction against what they saw as the dangers of extravagant Humean speculation. Kant himself rejected this common-sense philosophy as a mere 'appeal to the opinion of the multitude'. (And it's true that Kant's transcendental system is hardly vulnerable to *this* attack.)

In Britain, the second half of the nineteenth century belonged to the (Kantian and Hegelian) idealists, but in the last eighty years or so, common sense has made a comeback.

Do you agree . . . ?

1. **Thinking involves mental processes but not mental entities.**

2. **Any belief with Reid's 'three marks' is self-evident.**

3. **Philosophy cannot criticise common sense.**

4. **Perception of the external world is direct (not mediated by mental representations).**

CHAPTER 16

Universals

We now turn to another area profoundly affected by the rejection of causes-as-purposes. For Aristotle, the classifications we find embedded in language depend on final causes. In the present chapter, we look first at Plato's account of classification, and then at Aristotle's reaction against it.

We have been looking (since Chapter 11) at what happens to 'knowledge' if you change what you mean by 'cause'. I don't pretend for a moment that we've settled what happens, but in this chapter, I want to turn to a topic related to knowledge, the topic of classification.

What's the relation? Simply, that knowledge has seemed to many people to be impossible without classification. Kant was far from being the first to stress the importance of organising experience into categories or classes. It was one of the few things Plato and Aristotle agreed about, and I suppose that to many people it seems no more than common sense. Thomas Hobbes roundly claimed that 'By the advantage of [common] names it is that we are capable of science, which beasts, for want of them, are not'.

Imagine a new-born baby screwing up its eyes against the light. The baby is clearly getting sensory input. But what does it *know*? The temptation is to say 'Nothing at all', since even to say that it knows it doesn't like the light would, strictly speaking, seem to require that it knows what 'light' is. But on this first encounter, the baby doesn't know what light is (even in the very rough sense that you or I know). It simply screws up its eyes.

So it seemed to Plato and Aristotle, and to many others after them, that any account of knowledge must include an account of classification, or conceptualisation, or natural kinds, or general names, or whatever you want to call it. What, then, is the difference between simply screwing up your eyes and recognising light, between automatic response and *knowing*?

The problem of universals

For a couple of millennia, this problem was seen as a problem about 'universals'. People thought that when we classify, a particular thing is 'brought under' a universal, by means of which it can be lumped together with a whole lot of other particular things, forming a class. The question was: what exactly is the relation between a particular and the universal under which it falls? What relationship is it, for example, between a shape drawn in the sand and

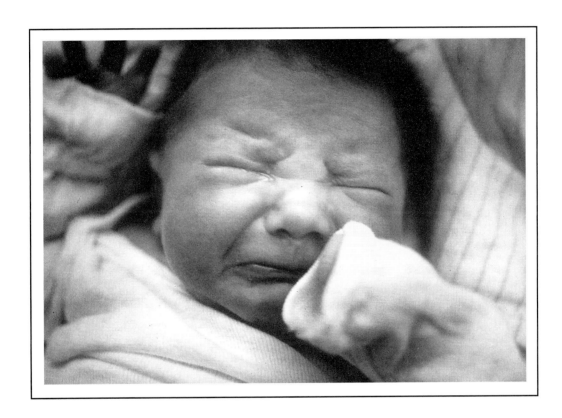

the universal 'TRIANGLE' which makes it true that the shape is a triangle? About sixteen hundred years ago, a Syrian called Porphyry (c.232–305) set out the options as he saw them. Universals might exist either independently, or in the mind. If they exist independently they might be either corporeal or incorporeal. Again, they might exist either *in* particular things, or else separated from them.

Now it's plausible to argue, following Plato, that we have never seen a perfect circle or triangle. Any geometrical figure we have seen has some drafting imperfections. In spite of this we can say that one figure is closer than another to being perfectly circular or triangular. We can also say, for example, that the internal angles of a (Euclidean) triangle amount to *exactly* 180 degrees, even though no triangle we have ever seen will actually measure 180.000 . . . degrees, even to the first thousand decimal places. It looks, then, as if we must have ideas of a perfect circle or triangle (and of perfect justice, beauty and everything else), which do not come to us from experience. So where do these ideas come from? Well, according to Plato, the soul recollects them from previous acquaintance with a realm (the realm of What Does Not Change) where these ideas exist. This, incidentally, proves that the soul is reincarnated.

Reasoning along these lines, Plato concluded that universals are incorporeal and exist independently of actual tables and chairs, horses and men (since these things belong in the realm of What Changes). Plato himself discovered problems in this account, and late in his life, rejected it. There's a problem, for example, about saying that something exists but does not change, because (as we said in Chapter 4) it's very tempting to explain existence in terms of causal role, which necessarily involves change.

Then again, Plato's account looks regressive. Suppose I come across a something-or-other and, thanks to my soul's acquaintance with the eternal idea of a horse, know it for a horse. Did I accomplish this by noticing a resemblance between the something and the idea? If no, how *did* I accomplish it? That is, how did I link the something with the eternal idea of a horse as opposed to the eternal idea of a carburettor? But if yes, and there's a resemblance between the something-or-other and the eternal idea of a horse (hereafter *horse) then we can make a new class, containing not just real live horses, but real live horses *plus* *horse. But on Plato's account, classes need corresponding eternal ideas, so there must be another eternal idea for this new class (call it **horse). Whereupon we can form another new class, containing all real live horses, plus *horse, plus **horse, which means there must be yet another eternal idea (***horse), and so on. This regress is probably more of an embarrassment than a real logical problem for Plato, because it's not clear that we need later members of the series in order to access earlier ones.

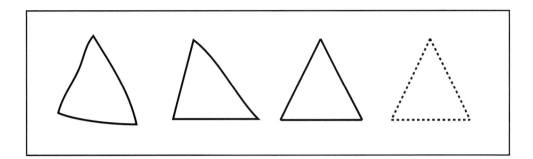

Plato explaining why we must have innate ideas:

'Suppose that you see something and you say to yourself, "This thing has a tendency to be like something else, but it falls short and is only a poor imitation." Don't you agree that anyone who has this thought must have previous knowledge of the thing which he says that the other inadequately resembles?' *Phaedo* (c.375 BC)

Perhaps Plato could in theory brazen it out by saying that there just *are* infinitely many eternal ideas. But the real function of the regress is to dramatise the fact that Plato's account depends on an unexplained notion of resemblance and so does not really advance our understanding of classification at all.

Aristotle on classification

Aristotle therefore proposed a different account, according to which the members of a class have in common, not an unexplained relationship to something external to the class, but a certain material organisation. The horses Shergar and Dobbin belong to the same class, because the matter out of which they are composed is organised in the same way. It's this organisational feature which makes something a horse. However, for Aristotle, 'organisation' isn't just a matter of shape or structure: it has something to do with function. Think of the hand of a corpse. This is obviously made of the same type of matter, organised in the same way, as the hand of a living person. But Aristotle insists that a dead hand is not a hand. It has lost the function of a hand. It doesn't do what hands are meant to do.

We might call this Aristotelian concept 'functional organisation' (though it's really another manifestation of the idea of a final cause – a dead hand no longer fulfils its natural *purpose*, which is to grasp). Aristotle's view, then, is that if two particular things have the same 'functional organisation', they belong to the same class. Returning to Porphyry's questions, we can say that for Aristotle, universals are (in a sense) *in* things. They certainly don't exist independently of things. And whether 'functional organisation' is corporeal or incorporeal is a tricky question which probably requires a clearer notion of 'corporeal' than Porphyry possessed.

In mediaeval times, Plato was said to hold that universals exist *ante rem* (before the thing), whereas Aristotle held that they exist *in rebus* (in things). Thomas Aquinas (1225–1274) attempted a splendid synthesis of these great authorities by saying that universals exist *ante rem* in the mind of God, *in rebus* in themselves, and *post rem* (after the thing) in the mind of man. In essence this adjudicates in favour of Aristotle. But it raises the question of the role of human psychology in classification. And in the mediaeval period, the theory that universals were human concepts gained ground.

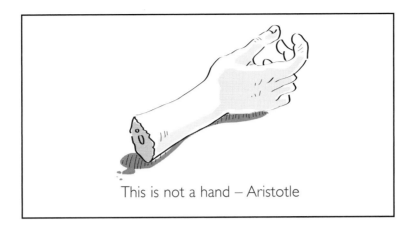

This is not a hand – Aristotle

Do you agree . . . ?

1. **No one has ever seen a perfect circle.**

   _____

2. **We do not get our idea of a perfect circle from experience.**

   _____

3. **There must be something which all horses have in common.**

   _____

4. **The only thing all horses have in common is that they all conform to our idea of a horse.**

   _____

CHAPTER 17

Abstraction

In this chapter, we look first at Locke's replacement for Aristotle's teleological account of classification, then at the more sophisticated accounts of Berkeley and Hume. It will be suggested that all three of these 'conceptualist' theories fail.

The mediaeval period saw intense debate about universals, and serious doubts about whether they had any basis in reality at all. We wind the clock forward to the seventeenth century, however, when the growing hostility to purpose in scientific explanations began to tell against Aristotle's theory of universals (as it had undermined his account of real or systematic knowledge). If everything that happens is to be explained in terms of causality understood as material impulse, then causal properties (devoid of purpose) should also be enough to classify the world.

Locke said that the 'direct and immediate signification' of a word is an idea in the mind of the user. He acknowledged that we do think of words as signifying things in the world (the word 'Bucephalus' denoting a particular horse for example), and he also knew that we take our words to correspond to ideas in the minds of all the other members of our language group. But he insisted that, first and foremost, the meaning of any word *I* use is an idea in *my* mind.

Locke on abstract ideas

Now obviously, the word 'Bucephalus' does not mean the same as the word 'horse'. So the idea in my mind which gives meaning to 'Bucephalus' must be different from the idea which gives meaning to 'horse'. Following the theory of Peter Abelard (1079–1142), Locke claimed that the difference between these two ideas is that my idea for the word 'horse' is more abstract than my idea for the word 'Bucephalus'. In fact, on Locke's theory, my 'horse' idea is formed out of the rich, particular ideas I have of 'Bucephalus', 'Dobbin', 'Shergar' etc. by *discarding* from them whatever is unique to each. My idea of 'Shergar', for example, might include a distinctive white blaze on the forehead. But when I use the word 'horse' I do not intend it to pick out only horses with a white blaze on the forehead, and so I jettison that and any other distinctive feature, and leave only a kind of schematic idea, which Locke calls an abstract general idea. According to Locke, it is thanks to my natural ability to create these abstract general ideas that I am able to use general words such as 'horse'.

Locke identifying
meanings with ideas:

'Words in their
primary or
immediate
signification, stand
for nothing, but the
Ideas in the Mind
of him that uses
them . . .' *Essay*
(1689)

. . . and general
meanings with
abstract general
ideas:

'Words become
general, by being
made the signs of
general *Ideas*: and
Ideas become
general, by
separating from
them the
circumstances of
Time, and place, and
any other *Ideas*, that
may determine them
to this or that
particular Existence.'
Essay (1689)

On this view, classification is made possible by a special kind of non-specific concept, a mental item which gives meaning to general words. This kind of theory, in various more or less sophisticated forms, continues to be popular today. One virtue is that it explains how we can generate the idea of a perfect triangle, for example, without ever having seen one. The drafting anomalies of the triangles we have actually seen, being unique to those particular examples, are omitted when we construct the abstract general idea of a triangle.

Now it's an interesting thing about triangles that there are exactly three kinds of triangle. Some are equilateral (their three sides are all the same length), some are isosceles (they have two sides the same length), and some are scalene (all three sides are different lengths). Anything which is a triangle is either equilateral, isosceles or scalene: and contrariwise, anything which is not equilateral, not isosceles and not scalene just isn't a triangle. Well, what about the abstract general idea of a triangle? It can't be an idea of an equilateral triangle (because if it were, the word 'triangle' would apply only to equilateral triangles). In the same way, it can't be an idea of an isosceles or scalene triangle. But if it's an idea of something not equilateral, not isosceles and not scalene, then as we saw a moment ago, it's an idea of something which is not a triangle at all.

This devastating criticism was made by Locke's usual nemesis, Berkeley. One attempt to salvage something from the wreckage points out that we *can* form non-specific ideas. If you ask someone to imagine a tiger for example, as vividly as they can, and then ask them how many stripes their tiger has, they will mostly laugh and say they have no idea. Of course a tiger has stripes and they knew that, but they just weren't thinking about the stripes. The image they formed was non-specific as to number of stripes. But as a defence of Locke, this misses the point. On Locke's account, equilateral-ness has to be definitely removed because it is distinctive of a sub-group of triangles, just as a white blaze on the forehead has to be removed from the abstract general idea of a horse. To suggest that we can be determinedly vague about the point is to suggest a new account.

Berkeley on classification

In fact, it is to suggest Berkeley's new account. Berkeley was quite rude about Locke's abstract general ideas, claiming that we haven't got any, can't make any, and wouldn't profit any if we could. Instead, we use specific ideas, such as the idea of Shergar, to give meaning to a general word like 'horse' and if there are any inconvenient features in the idea, such as that white blaze, we just ignore them. Berkeley also pointed out that we can use words without any idea at all

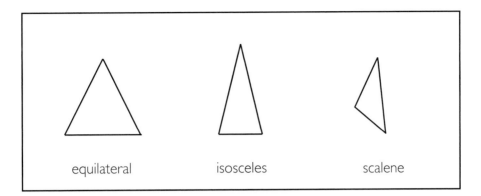

equilateral   isosceles   scalene

Locke (rashly) on the abstract idea of a triangle:

'...does it not require some pains and skill to form the general idea of a triangle (which is yet none of the most abstract, comprehensive and difficult); for it must be neither oblique nor rectangle, neither equilateral, equicrural, nor scalenon; but all and none of these at once.' *Essay* (1689)

Berkeley:

'...a man may *consider* a figure merely as triangular, without attending to the particular qualities of the angles, or relations of the sides.' *Principles of Human Knowledge* (1710)

actually coming to mind (which has led some people to think he was on the point of escaping from the whole meanings = ideas framework).

As an account of classification, however, I suppose the problem with Berkeley's theory is plain enough. How do we know which features are 'inconvenient'? Well, they're the ones which not all members of the class possess. So we must be able to say what the members of the class are, independently of the particular idea which, Berkeley claims, we use to determine this. At best, then, the way we use a particular idea might *express* the classification: it cannot explain how we arrive at it. The charitable line now is that this too supports the view that Berkeley realised that meanings are not ideas. But if Berkeley had really seen this, why would he have proposed the 'new account' just sketched?

Hume was very much impressed with Berkeley's theory of classification, and developed Berkeley's suggestion that ideas might not be necessary at the conscious level. (There was in fact quite a lot of talk about the unconscious before Freud, and in Hume particularly, unconscious processes such as mental association are central to our linguistic and more general cognitive abilities.) Thus, where Berkeley insisted that we cannot *remove* the inconvenient features of a particular idea, to form a Lockean abstract idea, but must instead *selectively ignore* them, Hume regards the particular idea which comes to mind when we use a general term as more or less irrelevant. The important thing is the activation of a 'custom', which acts as a kind of unconscious retrieval mechanism, drawing appropriate particular ideas from memory into consciousness, as we need them.

As an explanation of how we classify, this begs the question as openly as Berkeley's account did. To say that we can use and understand a general term such as 'triangle' because we have a mental retrieval mechanism which ranges over the ideas we have acquired of triangles, presupposes that all our ideas of triangles sit together neatly in a *class*. Which is what we set out to explain.

Hume on resemblance

But it was also Hume who (I suspect) indirectly put an end to the problem of universals. I think it's fair to say that not many philosophers now look for theories about what makes classification possible. The reason might be, for example, that psychology or linguistics or both have taken over the problem and are applying detailed empirical methods to it. Or it might be that the distinction we began with (between just screwing up your eyes and knowing that it's light) is breaking down, so that classification, as the means whereby we make that distinction, is no longer of such interest. But I think, most of all,

Hume:

A general word 'raises up an individual idea, along with a certain custom; and that custom produces any other individual [idea], for which we have occasion.' *Treatise* (1739)

that we have come to accept classification as something too basic to be explained.

Thus: the most common principle of classification seems to be resemblance, though as John Austin (1911–1960) pointed out, following Aristotle, classification can certainly proceed on other principles too. What is it to see a resemblance? In Hume's system, resemblance is fundamental to all reasoning about experience and all association of ideas and impressions. It is something we simply intuit, a basic aspect of our responsiveness to experience. The moral seems to be that resemblance lies too deep to be explained in terms of anything else.

If that's correct, we seem to have found our way back to Plato's taken-for-granted notion of resemblance (though without his dualist clothing for it) as the best we can do in explaining classification at the conceptual level. Of course there will be some physical implementation which makes seeing resemblances possible for us, and of course we can give examples of resemblances. There is also a question outstanding about the extent to which it is possible to *justify* the classes we find ourselves forming. But when pressed or tempted to give a definition of resemblance, if Hume is right, we just have to be strong – and say no.

Conclusion

To sum up: if we can't explain classification by reference to Aristotelian final causes (because we don't believe in final causes any more), then a promising alternative is to explain it by reference to concepts, whether special schematic concepts, specific concepts used in a general way, or a mental mechanism ranging over specific concepts. Like many promising alternatives before it, however, this 'conceptualism' quickly bites the dust. We've seen in this chapter that these conceptualist theories fail to explain what they set out to explain. Now in itself, this isn't so bad. Our ability to classify is so deeply involved in all our thinking that there's probably nothing deeper in terms of which we can give a general account of it. What's bad about conceptualist theories is that they hide this truth from us by giving a specious explanation, and further, that this specious explanation creates insoluble new problems. For example, if Locke says we all know introspectively that we have *lots* of abstract general ideas, and Berkeley says we haven't *any*, we have a problem: how do we decide who's right?

Family resemblances

Wittgenstein pointed out that we often classify things into a single group, not because they all have some single feature in common, but because they have several of some large set of features in common. Agatha, Beryl and Chloe might all have the Dangerfield family face, not because they all have the same eyes or the same chin, but because Agatha and Beryl have the eyes, while Beryl and Chloe have the chin. This implies that Agatha and Chloe might be classified together, even though they don't have any single feature in common. In Wittgenstein's splendid metaphor, 'the strength of the thread does not reside in the fact that some one fibre runs through its whole length, but in the overlapping of many fibres'.

This is a useful reminder, but it doesn't attempt to explain what resemblance is. What it says is that we often classify on the basis of multiple resemblances, rather than just one.

Do you agree . . . ?

1. **The meaning of a word is an idea in the mind of the speaker/hearer.**

2. **Human beings are naturally able to form abstract general ideas.**

3. **Berkeley's account of classification (and Hume's too) does not really explain it.**

4. **It is impossible to explain what resemblance is.**

CHAPTER 18

Names

The last two chapters explained the relevance of causes-as-purposes to classification in language. We continue to explore its importance for language, turning in the present chapter to proper names. Is it possible to explain how we use proper names if we have decided to reject the idea of purpose?

We saw in the last chapter Locke's claim that the meaning of a word is an idea in the mind of the user. In fact, there is a whole bunch of thorny problems here (known collectively as the Theory of Meaning), and we cannot really pass by without stopping to notice one or two of them. In this chapter, therefore, we're going to look at naming, and in the next, communication.

The problem of classification, or universals, could also be described as the problem of common names. 'Bucephalus' is a proper name: 'horse' is a common name. And Locke's approach was to take for granted our ability to use proper names, then ask what has to be different to explain our ability to use common names (the answer being, of course, that a different and rather special kind of idea is involved). But we can also think a bit more deeply about what Locke takes for granted. How do I use 'Bucephalus' – which after all is just a noise or a mark on paper – to name a particular thing? What underlies my ability to do this?

Names and mental representations

One account would go like this: the word 'Bucephalus' is just aural or visual input, but it gives rise in my mind to a mental representation of itself (or to be precise, to lots of them, since I've seen and heard the name on several occasions). These mental representations of the name are associated with various others, for example, with my mental representations of a painting I once saw, of things I have read about Alexander, of what my teachers told me about Macedonia, and so on. Taken together, these representations pick out only one horse in the whole of history. So I know that 'Bucephalus' stands for that particular horse.

Of course, I've never seen Bucephalus, and neither has anyone else now alive. So the mental representations which pick out Bucephalus are in a sense, derivative. In the case of Dobbin (who, let's suppose, I have seen) the mental representations which pick out Dobbin from everything else would include many which I have acquired directly, from perception.

Descartes too thought that our language abilities can be explained by ideas in the mind. He writes:

'...whenever I express something in words and understand what I am saying, this very fact makes it certain that there is within me an idea of what is signified by the words.' *Second Set of Replies* (1641)

Well, this gets us precisely nowhere, I suppose. My ability to link the name 'Bucephalus' with Bucephalus, or 'Dobbin' with Dobbin, is here explained by my ability to link one lot of mental representations with another lot. I link the 'Bucephalus' lot (which allow me to pick out that name from all my other visual and aural input), with the Bucephalus lot (which allow me to pick out that particular horse). This merely pushes the ability to link into a mysterious place (my mind) where nobody can examine it. It doesn't *explain* anything. On the contrary, it creates something else *to* explain, because not only do I have to link the 'Bucephalus' representations with the Bucephalus ones, I also have to link indefinitely many individual representations together to form these two lots. What's more, I have to know that the important thing about the 'Bucephalus' lot is that they exist to allow me to pick out the name 'Bucephalus' (rather than, for example, the syllables 'Bu-ceph'). How do I know this? Could it be, for example, that I create out of all these particular representations of 'Bucephalus', which I have heard in various accents and pronunciations, and seen in various hands and fonts, an abstract idea of the name 'Bucephalus'? This would be discouraging indeed, because explaining proper names was supposed to be easier than explaining common names, and yet now proper names seem to depend on classification after all.

A mental-representations account, then, seems to multiply problems instead of solving them. One response is to stop talking about mental representations and start talking about beliefs instead. We might say, for example, that I have one set of beliefs about the name 'Bucephalus' and another set of beliefs about the horse Bucephalus, and that I come to be able to use the name properly when I come to hold the linking belief that *that* name applies to *that* thing. This does nothing to solve the problem of explaining how all these beliefs get neatly sorted into the appropriate classes (without presupposing the ability to name, which is what the account is supposed to be explaining). And it raises another problem, which applies to both the mental representation-style and the belief-style account.

What does it *mean* to say that someone has a particular mental representation, or a particular belief? What does it mean to believe that fire burns, for example? Among many other things, it means not putting your hand into the fire, warning others about the dangers of fire, keeping important papers away from fire and so on. What, then, does it mean to say that someone possesses the linked 'Bucephalus'-Bucephalus representations or beliefs? Well of course, it means pointing to the horse in certain pictures (not for example, the rider, or a building in the background). It means answering 'Bucephalus' when asked to name Alexander the Great's favourite horse, and so on indefinitely. In other words, the ability to use the proper name explains what it is to have the representation or belief, not vice versa. Time, then, to look for a quite different kind of account.

Names and 'baptisms'

Consider how proper names are actually introduced into language. Someone steps up and says 'I name this child, or ship, or whatever-it-is, X'. Mum buys the kids a budgie and someone says 'Let's call it Chirrup' and so on. In short, there's usually a kind of naming ceremony, performed by someone who has some sort of right to decide the thing's name. Can we say, then, that being able to use the name is a matter of knowing about, or falling into line with, or being *somehow* connected to, the original naming ceremony? Some people have tried to characterise this connection between later users of the name and the original ceremony as a *causal* connection, and as a result, this account of naming is sometimes called the causal theory of names.

One advantage of this kind of account is that it explains how I can use a name when I don't have mental representations or beliefs detailed enough to pick out the thing I name. I can use the name Gilgamesh, for example, knowing only that Gilgamesh was the hero of a religious myth who went on a search for the secret of eternal life (hardly enough to pick out one individual), because I heard the name from people who are 'closer' to the naming ceremony than I am. If pressed for more detail, I can refer to them.

Another advantage can be brought out by the strange case of Napoleon's double. According to the beliefs or representations kind of account, the name 'Napoleon' refers to whoever happens best to fit the beliefs or representations associated with it. The reference of the name is determined by the beliefs or representations. Now let's suppose that, rather early in his career, Napoleon began to use a double. In this case, most of the beliefs or representations we associate with the name 'Napoleon' might really be true of Claude, his double, and not true of *him* at all. Does it follow that the name 'Napoleon' really refers to Claude? Not at all – the name refers to the man who (we now discover) used the double. It seems to follow that the reference of the name is fixed, not by means of any class of representations or beliefs, but by some kind of naming ceremony, such as Napoleon's baptism, and a 'chain of communication' from it to us.

A causal theory?

So the mental representations account gets into difficulties when a user's mental representations are not detailed enough to pick out a single individual, or not accurate enough to pick out the right individual. The so-called causal account – associated with the names of Saul Kripke (1940–) and Hilary Putnam (1926–) – avoids these problems, and it is also an improvement over the solipsism of earlier accounts: it presents language as a cooperative, communal thing, which must be good. However, two large questions remain to be answered. First, what must my relation be to the initial naming ceremony if

'Let's call him Scamp.'

A week later

'The Joneses have a dog,
you know. Scamp, I think.'

A decade later

'It just ran out in front of me.'
'Hmm, 'Scamp' it says on the collar.'

Several decades later

'I used to have a dog you know.
Now what did we call it?'

Evans on name and thing:

One interesting attempt to clarify the nature of the relation between someone who uses a name and the thing he or she names is due to Gareth Evans (1946–1980). Evans suggests that a name names that thing which is causally responsible for most of the information we associate with the name. There are certainly problems with this, and exceptions, as Evans points out. Most of the information we associate with the name 'Napoleon' might causally derive from Claude, for example. But the main point to notice here is that this account too depends on our *intentions* to use a sound as a name. Like Kripke before him, Evans realises that a purely causal account is too much to hope for. In short, if we want to understand how a sound names a thing, we need an explanation of what is involved in having an intention.

Russell, for example, claimed that 'The relation of a word to its meaning is of the nature of a causal law governing our use of the word and our actions when we hear it used' (*The Analysis of Mind*, 1921).

139

I am to be able to use the name? And second, what is it about that initial ceremony which establishes the sound as a name?

It's hard to see any successful answer to these questions in purely causal terms. The same causal relations might hold between all parties when people decide *not* to accept a given name as the thing's name. A pretender might go through a ceremony of being named king (as the 'Old Pretender' was named James III), and the appropriate, purely causal relations between namer, thing named and audience might obtain, without 'James III' becoming James Edward Stuart's name. Names become fixed because people *accept* them, and this acceptance depends (in many cases) on their perceiving the namer as having the *right* to give the name. But it's hard to see how we might explain rights in purely causal terms (unless final causes are considered respectable again).

So perhaps we should say that the essential thing about the ceremony is the participants' *intention* to use that sound as the thing's name hereafter. Correspondingly, the relation I must stand in to the initial naming ceremony is that I must defer to that intention (that is, must conform my own intention in using the sound to that of the original namer, whatever his or her intention was). In this case, we are taking it for granted that we understand what it is to intend to use a sound as a name. But isn't this where we came in? The mental representations account would now insist that to form such an intention is a matter of linking the 'Chirrup' lot of representations with the Chirrup lot, so that we need to return to the mental representations account after all.

Conclusion

What this means is that there are really two separate issues here. One is whether the reference of a proper name is normally fixed by *descriptions* which users associate with the name, or by some act of baptism, based essentially on pointing. A second issue is whether 'associating' (either names with descriptions or names directly with things) should be understood in terms of linked classes of mental representations. My own opinion would be that the reference of a proper name is usually fixed by an initial baptism and by later speakers deferring to the intentions of those who originally gave the name. On the second issue, I claimed that talk about mental representations cannot *explain* what it is to form an intention or make an association. We'll consider the question of how we *should* explain such things in Chapter 21.

But however we understand intending or associating, the fact remains that the so-called causal theory depends on them as much as its rival does. The causal theory of names was eagerly interpreted as promising to explain naming in terms of *correlations* between the usages of people at different stages in the chain of communication – and this would clearly be a great contribution to the programme of eliminating final causes. But after all, it seems that the users' purposes are irreducible.

Searle on names:

The chief contemporary defender of a mental-representations account has been John Searle (1932–). In his book *Intentionality*, he argues that in causal theories too, 'reference is secured in virtue of . . . content in the mind of the speaker', because the important thing is that the speaker *intends* to use the name in the same way as the person who forms the previous link in the chain of communication. This assumes that having an intention is a matter of having certain content in one's mind.

Searle (following Evans) also argues that if the reference of the name is fixed, not by this mental content, but by whatever the chain of communication happens to lead to, then the name 'Madagascar', for example, refers to part of the mainland of Africa, not to the large island off the east coast. Apparently, Marco Polo misunderstood his informant (the person before him in the chain). Marco Polo took the name to refer to the island when in fact it referred to part of the mainland. So if 'Madagascar' refers to the island, as we all now think, that proves (according to Searle) that the reference of the name is not fixed by the initial baptism, but by the content we now have in mind when we use it.

Do you agree . . . ?

1. **Knowing the name of a mountain, for example, is a matter of mentally associating the mountain with the name.**

   _____

2. **Naming must be social because it involves the right to name and rights are always social.**

   _____

3. **Intending to use a certain sound as a name is a matter of mentally resolving to do so.**

   _____

CHAPTER 19

Communication

In this chapter, we turn to the essential 'purpose' of language – communication. Is it possible to explain communication in any scientific way, if science fundamentally rejects explanations which depend on the idea of purpose?

What happens when you catch my drift (assuming that you sometimes do)? Ideas may have let us down over common names and proper names, but surely here, we feel, they can help. When I want to say something, I have some idea which I want to get across to you. I can't transplant it directly into your mind, but (happily for both of us) I can communicate it indirectly, through language. I put my idea into words, utter them, and when you hear them, you convert the words back into an idea. In this admittedly roundabout way, you end up with the same idea in your mind that I had in mine – and that's communication.

This was certainly Locke's theory, and we find it again in 'the father of modern linguistics', Ferdinand de Saussure. The same theory continues to thrive today (alas).

Saussure on communication

Saussure added three interesting new wrinkles to this venerable picture of communication. The picture tends to suggest, for example, that ideas exist prior to language, perfectly formed and complete. The point of language is only to make them public. Saussure held on the contrary that without language, our concepts would be chaotic and indistinct. Language gives them not only expression but stability, distinctness and indeed meaning.

The picture also suggests, secondly, that communication occurs between senders and receivers working essentially in isolation. I formulate my message in the solitude of my own mind, put it into a coded form which others might in theory detect, and send it off into the void. Saussure, by contrast, tries to do justice to the social nature of language by stressing that no solitary individual could invent language. The conventions on which language is based can only develop in a community (though Saussure unfortunately doesn't explain why this is so).

The third of Saussure's wrinkles is the most complex. The picture suggests that each word is given meaning individually, by connection with an idea or

Saussure (1857–1913) on the holistic nature of meaning:

'If words stood for pre-existing concepts, they would all have exact equivalents in meaning from one language to the next; but this is not true ...

When they are said to correspond to concepts, it is understood that the concepts are purely differential and defined not by their positive content but negatively by their relations with the other terms of the system. Their most precise characteristic is in being what the others are not.' *Course in General Linguistics* (1916)

concept (a claim we saw explicitly in Locke). The mere sound becomes a sign by standing for a concept – and Saussure himself endorses this picture at first. Later, however, he emphasises that the meaning of a given word depends on the other words around it in the language. For Saussure, the meaning of 'red' in English, for example, is defined by its contrasts with 'brown', 'orange', 'yellow', 'purple' etc. Thus, in a language which had only one word for 'orange' and 'yellow', there *could not be* a word exactly equivalent to the English word 'red'. Some of Saussure's statements of this idea are so extreme as to be paradoxical, but he did at least want to stress that the meaning of a word comes not only from its association with a concept, but also from its role in a framework of other words.

All three of these Saussurean ideas look plausible. All three remedy weaknesses in the original Lockean account. Unfortunately, neither they nor anything else can solve the basic problem with such an account.

Idiom or explanation?

Remember that the account is supposed to explain what constitutes success in communication. Communication has succeeded when the receiver has the same ideas in mind that the sender had. Now, how do we check that their ideas really are the same? According to Locke, the sender's ideas 'are all within his own breast, invisible and hidden from others, nor can of themselves be made to appear'. This is precisely why a public medium like language is necessary. But if the *receiver's* ideas are 'invisible and hidden from others', all we can check is that he or she behaves in the desired or expected way, answers to the point, and so on. In this case, 'having the same ideas in mind' is not something we can establish independently of communicative success. On the contrary, we have to use communicative success as the criterion of 'having the same ideas in mind'. What this means is that 'having the same ideas in mind' is an *idiom for*, not an *explanation of*, communicative success. It's another way of saying that A and B have succeeded in communicating, not an explanation of what made their success possible.

Think about 'catching someone's drift'. No one would suggest as an *explanation* of the fact that A has succeeded in communicating something to B, that B has caught A's drift. Why not? Because nobody thinks drifts have real existence. But, thanks to Descartes and Locke, people do think ideas have real existence, and so they take the 'same ideas' idiom literally, and conjure up from it a kind of mechanism which explains communication.

If this is right, then although we can go on saying that A and B are two minds with but a single thought, that they have the same idea, that B doesn't get the idea, and all the rest of it, we have to understand these expressions as

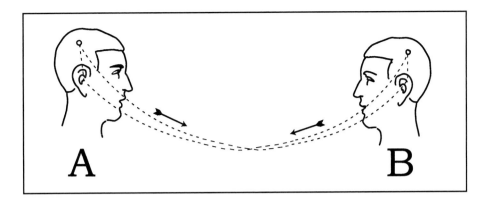

Communication – according to Saussure (or his editors)

Three kinds of processes are involved: *physical* processes of producing and receiving changes in air pressure, *physiological* processes between brain and ear or mouth, and *psychological* processes of associating sounds as they appear to the mind with concepts.

Explanatory metaphor

It's easy to mistake an idiom for an explanation because there's an important animal which looks a bit like both – the explanatory metaphor.

If we say an electron *orbits* the nucleus, or if we say memory is a *storehouse* of ideas, or if we call DNA a *code*, these are metaphors which at a certain stage might be important for unifying what we know and suggesting new avenues for research. Even though, at a later stage, they will almost certainly become misleading, explanatory metaphors do seem, at the earlier stage, to provide or at least suggest genuine explanations.

Idioms are different, however. 'Getting one's ideas across' does not explain communication, any more than 'knocking someone's socks off' explains making a good impression. 'Intelligence' is not a cause of problem-solving, any more than 'kicking the bucket' is a cause of death. To put it very simply, an idiom which *says* X does not thereby *explain* X.

idioms. To interpret them as explanations is a misunderstanding, like misreading the 'catching someone's drift' idiom as an embryonic theory.

What should we look to, then, in order to explain success in communication? Here we can go in two directions, towards macro-explanation or micro-explanation. At the macro-level we can say that two people can succeed in communicating when they speak the same language, hold the same basic beliefs about the world, and have the same basic goals. If any of these conditions is not met, communication becomes at least more difficult.

Let's think a little more about the first of these conditions. What is it for two people to speak the same language? If we hope for a paper definition here, we will certainly be disappointed. English and Japanese are very different languages. French and Italian are different, but not quite so different. Spanish and Catalan are closer still. Scottish and Irish Gaelic can equally well be described as different languages or different dialects of the same language. There will even be differences between the linguistic knowledge possessed by two people who speak the same dialect, have been to the same school and have lived all their lives in the same street. There is no point in this continuum of differences which objectively demands to be seen as the knife-edge – on one side the same language, on the other side different ones. Does this mean that our question (what is it for two people to speak the same language?) is unanswerable? Not at all. We simply say that two people speak the same language when they use more or less the same words, more or less the same grammar, and more or less the same pronunciation. And if anyone worries about the 'more or less' in all this, we resort to examples, as above, to make clear what we mean.

A science of meaning?

There are certainly some interesting issues arising from this kind of macro-explanation. For example, some twentieth-century philosophers are impressed by the fact, if it is a fact, that interpreting a new language (or by parity of reasoning a familiar one) requires us to conjecture meanings, beliefs and goals simultaneously. When we are trying to figure out what someone means, we have to figure out at the same time what he or she believes and wants. But it's possible to argue that if these three – meanings, beliefs and purposes – cannot be treated separately, then (since science proceeds by isolating what it studies) they cannot be treated scientifically. Another argument to the same conclusion is that if goals (final causes) are inextricably involved in semantics, psychology, and economics, then no purely mechanical or correlational branch of science can deal with them. But if facts are what science dishes up, then whatever

Language-families

Confining ourselves to the languages of Central America, we find six main language-families (along with other languages which originated North or South). One of these families – by no means the largest – is Mayan, which includes about eighty distinguishable, related, languages. These eighty can be grouped into five Mayan sub-families, depending on their degree of relatedness.

But in fact the whole business is very controversial, in several ways. Many of these languages are extinct or moribund and/or poorly documented. Methods of measuring degrees of relatedness are very much open to challenge. And experts believe that almost all these languages had a common ancestor in prehistoric times.

In view of all this, it's easy to sympathise with the claim that to call something a separate language – based on its grammatical and phonological distinctness – is as much a political decision as a statement of fact. And of course, facts about *meaning* seem even harder to come by than facts about grammar or phonology. So the claim that there are no real facts about meaning, surprising though it is to common sense, seems to have some basis in the very real difficulties of language taxonomy.

science cannot present is not a fact. It follows that there are no facts about meaning.

A further point to notice, while we are considering macro-explanations of communication, is that Locke's account aspires to a quasi-causal system of correlations between words and ideas, a psychological *mechanism*. When I hear a word, the right idea comes to mind in some more or less automatic, unreasoned way. (No doubt it's this automatism which led Descartes and others to exempt their knowledge of language from the things they professed to doubt.) But this merely correlational linkage between words and ideas has to be supplemented (it seems) by guiding intentions in the use of words. Paul Grice (1913–1988), for example, places the speaker's intentions at the heart of the process of communication, identifying the meaning of what the speaker says with the complex of intentions which led to the saying of it. Roman Jacobson (1896–1982) said that 'the most striking feature of poetic language is its teleological character', and made this the basis of a system of language classification which was in conscious opposition to 'those who consider teleology synonymous with theology'. The moral seems to be, as it was when we looked at naming, that our existing concepts of language and language-use cannot do without the notion of purpose, without those bad old final causes.

Micro-explanation of success in communicating looks to brain research. It might turn out (though it quite probably won't) that knowing the meaning of a word, for example, will depend in a regular way on some recurring and identifiable state of the brain. The sensible thing to do here is wait and see.

Quine on translation:

The philosopher who has done most to emphasise the difficulties of radical translation — and consequently the unscientific nature of meaning — is Willard Quine. Quine imagines a field linguist trying to understand a completely unknown language, and claims that:

'Manuals for translating one language into another can be set up in divergent ways, all compatible with the totality of speech dispositions, yet incompatible with one another.' *Word and Object* (1960)

It's sometimes said that different scientific theories can be devised, which are equally compatible with all the evidence. Quine's view is that the translation manuals are in a worse fix, because in the language case, there are no facts lying as it were behind the evidence, to make one translation rather than the other true. For Quine, there are no real facts about meaning.

Do you agree . . . ?

1. **Successful communication occurs when the hearer gets the speaker's idea.**

   _____

2. **Exact translation from one language to another is mostly impossible.**

   _____

3. **Goals cannot be explained purely in terms of correlations.**

   _____

4. **There cannot be thought without language.**

   _____

CHAPTER 20

Perception

In this chapter, we return to Locke's ideational theory of perception (sketched in Chapter 12) and see how Locke's distinction between primary and secondary qualities gives rise to another problem for common sense.

We've spent the last few chapters looking into the usefulness of ideas, and I've been suggesting that, first appearances to the contrary, they haven't any. The source and origin of ideas (for an empiricist) is of course perception, and in understanding perception, ideas once again promise much. Let's see, then, what they deliver.

We know that there is a complex series of processes between the thing seen and the seeing of it. Light has to be reflected or emitted, to travel to the perceiver's eyes, to be focussed onto the retina, to stimulate nerve receptors there, and the resulting nerve signals have to travel along rather well-defined pathways in the brain to the visual cortex at the back of the head, where things get *really* complicated. If any of these processes of transmission go wrong, the perceiver won't see whatever-it-is.

We also know that, just as things can exist without being seen, so 'seeings' can occur without any thing there to be seen. When someone sees an after-image, he or she sees the shape of a window or candle flame or light where no window, candle flame or light exists. Few people would be fooled by an after-image, but people can indeed be fooled by hallucinations. Evelyn Waugh, for example, wrote *The Ordeal of Gilbert Pinfold* after his own experience of hearing very realistic voices. Martin Luther saw devils. In these cases, it seems, the later stages of normal transmission occur without the usual earlier stages.

Contents of experience

Let's concentrate on the last stages in the process of transmission. We have all sorts of brain activity spreading out from the visual cortex, and we have a subjective 'content of experience', like the after-image. Historically, there have been two main models of this final, subjective stage. The minority view has been that what happens here is a *modification* of consciousness: the stream of consciousness is changed in a particular way. We saw a version of this view in Reid's reaction against Hume.

The majority view holds, by contrast, that the after-image (for example) is

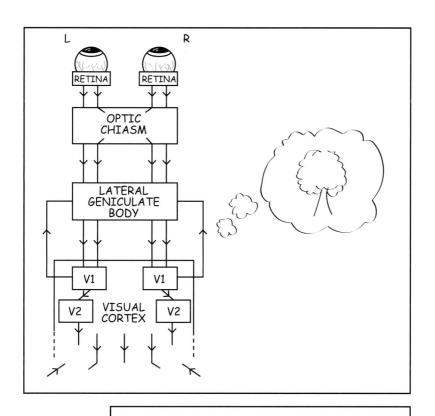

The Visual System . . .
and the Seeing of a Thing . . .
and the Thing Seen

an *object* of consciousness. It is something we are conscious of, not a way of being conscious. And we do say 'I see an after-image', just as we say 'I see a tree', encouraging the majority tendency to regard the after-image (and by extension the contents of other sensory experiences) as a kind of thing. If it's the grammatical object of the verb 'to see', why shouldn't it be the real object of the process of seeing? Since a general term for these objects would obviously be handy, we can call them – um – ideas.

Does that seem like common sense? Locke certainly thought so, and he used this model both to make a number of points about perception, and to bridge the gap between perceiving and thinking. Perceiving and thinking involve the same objects (ideas), but the first is a matter of passive reception, the second (whether in language or out of it) a matter of active manipulation.

Primary and secondary qualities

One of the main points Locke wanted to make about perception was that there is a difference between what he called primary and secondary qualities. Suppose I see a child's wooden block. The block has a certain shape, a cube let's say, and a certain colour, choose your favourite. Now these qualities of shape and colour are different from each other in some interesting ways. Shape can be seen and also discerned by touch, whereas colour is available only to sight. Again, shape can be specified mathematically by way of line lengths and internal angles. Perceived colour, on the other hand, cannot be specified mathematically (though reflected or emitted light can of course be quantified). Thirdly, it seems (or seemed to Galileo) that it is possible to imagine an object with no colour, but quite impossible to imagine an object with no shape. These differences between colour and shape have seemed sufficient to many people to show that qualities like shape are objective or real, whereas qualities like colour are subjective or 'secondary'. Newton went so far as to say about the ray of light in his famous prism experiments, 'the ray has no colours'.

Locke suggested that the difference between primary and secondary qualities can be understood in terms of *resemblance* between the idea of an object and the object itself: ideas of primary qualities resemble their causes, ideas of secondary qualities don't. Both kinds of idea are caused by features of the object, but these causally active features are all primary. Thus, our idea of the shape of the child's wooden block is a likeness of the block's real shape. Our idea of the colour of the block is not. It's caused, not by any colour in the block, but by certain (primary) qualities of the micro-texture of the block's surface.

We objected before (in Chapter 12) to claims about resemblance where it

Locke on primary and secondary qualities:

'Qualities thus considered in bodies are, first such as are utterly inseparable from the body, in what estate soever it be; such as in all the alterations and changes it suffers . . . it constantly keeps.

Secondly, such *qualities*, which in truth are nothing in the objects themselves but powers to produce various sensations in us by their *primary qualities*, i.e. by the bulk, figure, texture and motion of their insensible parts, as colours, sounds, tastes, etc. These I call *secondary qualities* . . .

. . . the *ideas of primary qualities* of bodies, *are resemblances* of them, and their patterns do really exist in the bodies themselves; but the *ideas produced* in us by these *secondary qualities, have no resemblance* of them at all.' *Essay* (1689)

Descartes ditto:

'In bodies we call "coloured" the colours are nothing other than the various ways in which the bodies receive light and reflect it against our eyes.' *Optics* (1637)

Galileo ditto:

'I think that tastes, odours, colours, and so on are no more than mere names so far as the object in which we place them is concerned, and that they reside only in the consciousness. Hence if the living creature were removed, all these qualities would be wiped away and annihilated.' *The Assayer* (1623)

is in principle impossible to get access to one of the terms of the alleged resemblance, but let's waive that problem here. The immediate question is: are we to accept this affront to common sense? Is it correct to say that the block has no colour? That lemons have no taste? That the big bass drum makes no sound, and so on?

Berkeley (self-appointed defender of common sense) dug his heels in here, and carried the fight back to Locke by claiming that whatever arguments might show that there are no secondary qualities out there in the world, could be adapted to show exactly the same thing about primary qualities. Leading – since the external world now has no qualities left – to idealism once again.

Locke had used this neat argument, for example. Suppose that there are three bowls of water in front of you, one cold, one lukewarm and one hot. You put your left hand in the cold water and your right hand in the hot. You leave them for a minute then put both hands into the lukewarm water. The lukewarm water now feels hot to the hand which was previously in the cold water, and cold to the hand which was previously in the hot water. But the same bowl of water can't be both hot and cold. So 'hot' and 'cold' aren't properties which really belong to the water. They're 'interactional' properties (to coin a term), which arise only when the water interacts with our sensory apparatus. Some primary quality of the water (the kinetic energy of the water molecules, as we now know) causes the sensations of hot and cold in us.

Locke also uses the example of a piece of coloured marble. Darken the room and the colour vanishes. But can the change of lighting cause any real change in the marble? No, says Locke. So its colour is not something *in* the marble, not a property belonging to the marble. It's a secondary quality, which arises only through a complex interaction involving the marble, light and human visual systems.

Dependent and independent qualities

These plausible arguments show the dependence of what we experience on the state of our sensory apparatus, or the state of the medium between the thing and us. Prepare our sensory apparatus in some way, or change the medium and naturally, what we experience will change. But this is equally true of motion or shape. If you accelerate quickly to thirty mph, that speed feels fast. Decelerate to thirty from sixty mph and it feels slow. But the same speed can't be both fast and slow. So 'fast' and 'slow' aren't real properties of things. And of course, if you switch the light off, the marble no longer looks square or Venus de Milo-shaped. Why doesn't this show that shape is as secondary as colour?

One response is to say that even with the light off, you could *feel* the shape

Cold   Lukewarm   Hot

Locke on colour:

'Can anyone think any real alterations are made in the porphyry by the presence or absence of light, when it is plain *it has no colour in the dark*?' *Essay* (1689)

The Venus de Milo
(in perfect darkness)

(primary qualities being accessible to more than one sense). Hence the interest of the 'Molyneux problem' (put to Locke in 1688 by an Irish doctor called William Molyneux). A person born blind could learn to distinguish by touch between a cube and a sphere. Suppose that, with the cube and the sphere both present, the person suddenly becomes able to see. Could he or she tell, without touching, which is the cube and which the sphere? Locke, Berkeley and Molyneux himself all thought the answer would be no. But if we have to *learn* the correlation between felt shape and seen shape, it's less clear that one and the same quality is really accessible to two senses.

A response to the motion problem is to concede that 'fast' and 'slow' may be subjective assessments, but insist that miles per hour, or centimetres per second, are objective properties really true of the thing which is moving. Speed, in this objective sense, can be tested by vision or by contact, and can be expressed in numbers. And so it remains a primary quality. Unfortunately, this common sense response is inconsistent with our best current science. Quantum theory implies, in effect, that vision *is a kind of* contact, so that any observation affects the thing observed. Relativity holds that speed can only be measured relative to a frame of reference, so that the Newtonian notion of absolute speed is empty. There is no 'real' speed at which a given object is moving.

Where does this leave Locke's distinction between primary and secondary qualities? It's enough of an affront to common sense that colour and the other secondary qualities are 'interactional'. If *all* properties are interactional, isn't that idealism, again, in scientific dress? Bohr's dictum – that no elementary phenomenon *is* a phenomenon until it is registered or observed by its macroscopic effects – looks very like a subatomic version of Berkeley's claim that to be is to be perceived. Bohr's colleague, the physicist J. A. Wheeler (1911–) says, 'Useful as it is under everyday circumstances to say that the world exists "out there" independent of us, that view can no longer be upheld. There is a strange sense in which this is a "participatory universe".' And Richard Feynman (1918–1988), deviser of quantum electrodynamics, says plainly that 'the price of gaining an accurate theory . . . has been the erosion of our common sense'. (That's 'erosion' as in 'utter and complete collapse'.)

B. K. Ridley on the interactional nature of reality:

'. . . the elementary particles cannot be put neatly into separate display cases and labelled confidently as this or that. Their natures are intimately bound up with their interactions with one another. Interactions involve the dynamic quantities energy and momentum (linear and angular), and these in turn involve mass and space and time. And now we really get into trouble, because to learn about mass and space and time we have to use elementary particles and their interactions with one another.' *Time, Space and Things* (1976)

Hermann von Helmholtz (1821–1894) on colour:

'. . . if what we call a property always implies an action of one thing on another, then a property or quality can never depend upon the nature of the agent alone, but exists only in relation to, and dependent on, the nature of some second object, which is acted upon. Hence, there is really no meaning in talking of properties of light which belong to it absolutely, independent of all other objects, and which we may expect to find represented in the sensations of the human eye. The notion of such properties is a contradiction in itself. They cannot possibly exist, and therefore we cannot expect to find any coincidence of our sensations of colour with qualities of light.' *Popular Lectures on Scientific Subjects* (1865–1871)

Do you agree . . . ?

1. **If there were no eyes there would be no colours.**

   _____

2. **We have to learn to correlate felt shape and seen shape.**

   _____

3. **There is no real distinction between primary and secondary qualities.**

   _____

4. **A property or quality can never depend on the nature of the object alone.**

   _____

CHAPTER 21

Life without Ideas

Instead of regarding human actions as the effects of mental causes (given the problems this seems to create), we might adopt one of three other theories: behaviourism, mind/brain identity, or functionalism. The first two need only correlational causality, but the third (currently and understandably the most popular) quietly reintroduces the concept of a final cause.

Locke's distinction between primary and secondary qualities was a distinction between what's really out there, and what's only in our heads. I softened that into a distinction between qualities which do not, and those which do, depend on interaction with human sensory apparatus. But the same fundamental problem seems to arise for this softened version too: the reasons for accepting that *some* real-seeming properties (the secondary or interactional ones) are not really 'out there', seem on reflection to apply to the so-called primary or 'non-interactional' properties too. How could we know that a property is non-interactional if all our knowledge *of* it is a kind of interaction *with* it?

Now we can certainly try to stem this tide of subjectivity. We can argue that there are degrees of dependence on interaction, and that although colour is *more* dependent than shape, this does not imply the shocking conclusion that tomatoes are not red – or if it does, it does not imply the even more shocking conclusion that tomatoes are not round. We can allow that *absolute* independence of interaction might be impossible, but to try to show that this falls short of idealism. There is, to put it mildly, a lot of scope for work along these lines.

But we should at least consider a radical alternative. Think back. What have ideas achieved for us? Created the insoluble problem of showing that other people have them. Created the equally impossible problem of understanding how they affect and are affected by the body. Failed to explain classification, naming and communication. And now, reduced the objective world to a human artifact, more or less. This is an impressive catalogue of disasters, and surveying it, we might well be inclined to ask if we can possibly do without ideas.

Ways of doing without ideas

In Chapter 15, we looked at Reid's attempt to eliminate ideas in favour of mental activities, but this still traps us in the private, interior world of the mind, and it was this privacy which caused most of the disasters listed above. So if we decide to reject ideas *and* mental activities in one fell swoop, what can

IDEAS

problems $\begin{cases} \text{SOLIPSISM} \\ \text{INTERACTION} \\ \text{IDEALISM} \end{cases}$

failures $\begin{cases} \text{NAMING} \\ \text{CLASSIFICATION} \\ \text{COMMUNICATION} \end{cases}$

The behaviourist B. F. Skinner on inner causes:

'. . . it is obvious that the mind and the ideas (which are used to explain behaviour), together with their special characteristics, are being invented on the spot to provide spurious explanations . . . Since mental or psychical events are asserted to lack the dimensions of physical science, we have an additional reason for rejecting them.' *Science and Human Behaviour* (1965)

we use instead of them to make sense of human beings? There are three main candidates: overt behaviour, brain states and functional states.

The great attraction of behaviourism (apart from the fact that it neglects or denies ideas) is that we base our beliefs about other people's mental lives on what they say and do. It's because someone winces, says 'My tooth hurts', goes to see a dentist, and so on, that we believe that he or she has toothache. So it's tempting to suppose that when we're trying to explain what people do, all that can really concern us is overt behaviour. Any apparent references to 'inner' causes (like beliefs, intentions and desires) must be shorthand for, or must be able to be cashed out in terms of, outer behaviour. To say that obsessional actions are caused by an unconscious desire, for example, must really be to say that the sufferer behaves in such a way as to secure some object, but also explicitly denies wanting whatever-it-is and repeats the actions in spite of securing the object.

The great attraction of brain states, on the other hand, is that the real causal explanation of what people do seems to lie there. Saying 'My tooth hurts', for example, is a matter of complex muscular movements involving the lungs, larynx and mouth, caused by signals passed along the relevant nerves from the brain. Brain states are not the evidence we presently use in explaining what people do, but they do look like the evidence we might ideally use. And of course it's always tempting – as with behaviourism – to reinterpret claims which seem problematic (about ideas) in terms of the evidence we have, or might ideally have, for making them. Concentrating on the evidence seems not only to detach and discard the problematic claims, but to be a way of getting down to essentials. It's also respectably empiricist, because the old empiricist doctrine that all our concepts come to us through experience can be rephrased as the claim that the meaning of a statement can't amount to anything more than the evidence we might have for asserting it.

The reality of experience

The great problem with both views, however, is that we seem to directly experience the thing they deny. In our own case, at least, we seem to know beyond all doubt that there is something more than overt behaviour and brain states. Intentions, decisions, beliefs, plans, perceptions and all the rest seem, from the inside, to be much more than just behaviour and/or brain states.

What's more, this is not a purely selfish point – we attribute experiences to others too. When I say George has toothache, I *don't* just mean that he says his tooth hurts, holds his jaw and goes to the dentist. I mean he has the kind of unpleasant sensations which I have when *I* have toothache. Indeed, this attribution of experiences to others is so well-entrenched, that I am perfectly willing to attribute experiences quite different from any of mine, to creatures

Ryle (1900–1976) on belief:

'...to believe that the ice is dangerously thin is to be unhesitant in telling oneself and others that it is thin ... it is also to be prone to skate warily, to shudder ... to warn other skaters.' *The Concept of Mind* (1949)

U. T. Place:

'"Consciousness is a process in the brain" is a reasonable scientific hypothesis, in the way "Lightning is a motion of electric charges" is a reasonable scientific hypothesis.' *Is Consciousness a Brain Process?* (1956)

which can't tell me anything about them. In a well-known essay, Thomas Nagel (1937–) considered the echo-location system used by bats – a sensory system we humans do not possess. We know what it's like to see colours and hear sounds, but we have no idea what it's like to detect cave walls, flying insects and what-not by their echoes. In spite of this, we are strongly inclined to think that echo-location has some associated 'quality of experience' in bat consciousness, just as sound and colour do in human consciousness. The question Nagel posed in 1974 – 'What is it Like to be a Bat?' – has a real answer, we tend to suppose, in spite of the fact that this answer is probably something we cannot discover, or even imagine.

All this is now called the problem of qualia – 'qualia' being a jargon term for subjective qualities of experience. It's a problem for all three of our alternatives to ideas (overt behaviour, brain states and functional states) because all three systematically overlook or deny the existence of qualia, though we seem firmly committed to them both in our own experience and in our thinking about others.

Functionalism

So far, we've looked briefly at the first two alternatives to ideas – overt behaviour and brain states. Let's turn now to the third and currently most popular – functional states. What, first of all, is a 'functional state'? Suppose a computer performs some useful function for you, such as calculating your taxes or storing some text. In performing this function, it does of course go through a series of very complicated physical states. So many milliamps pass along *this* bit of etched circuit board. Such-and-such resistors get slightly warmer over *there*. And so on, in as much detail as you have patience for. But in a sense, none of that matters very much. Of course, if that stuff didn't happen, the computer wouldn't do the things you want. But a different computer could perform the same functions for you, could store, calculate and all the rest, with a very different design of circuit board, different values and arrangements of resistors, even a quite different technology (such as valves instead of transistors). In fact, the kind of description an electronics expert or a physicist might give of what is happening (in terms of the interactions of electrons and electronic parts) would positively *obscure* what the computer is doing for you. It would tell you too much of the wrong sort of thing – as atomistic explanations almost always do. What we usually want, instead, is the kind of description a software engineer or systems analyst would give, in terms of following a programme or working through a flow-chart of functions. To come to the point at last, functionalism claims that the important thing for explaining what *people* do is, in the same way, the functional state of the whole system, not the physical state of the brain.

Colourless Mary

Imagine a baby – little Mary – brought up in a room containing only shades of grey. Her food is greyed-out artificially and the people she meets wear grey make-up. As she grows older, she learns about the world through books (none of which have colour pictures) and a black and white TV.

Now suppose that Mary masters the whole of science. She knows everything science has to teach her. She knows, for example, that tomatoes grow and ripen, and she knows that people call unripe tomatoes 'green', and ripe tomatoes 'red'.

By way of a reward, she is released from the colourless room and actually sees some ripe and unripe tomatoes. 'Wow!' she says, 'Look at that!' Doesn't she now know something she didn't know before? Doesn't she now know how ripe and unripe tomatoes *look*? But if she gains in knowledge, that seems to imply that there's a kind of fact which the scientific account missed out. The scientific facts she learned about tomatoes missed out the impressive 'qualia facts' which she now becomes aware of.

The case of colourless Mary is another way to dramatise the 'reality' of qualia.

Putnam:

'. . . two systems can have quite different constitutions and be functionally [identical]'. *Philosophy and our Mental Life* (1973)

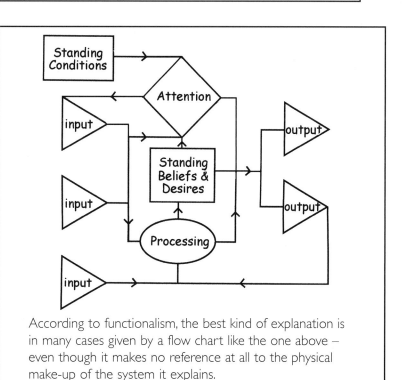

According to functionalism, the best kind of explanation is in many cases given by a flow chart like the one above – even though it makes no reference at all to the physical make-up of the system it explains.

163

Notice that our old friend purpose seems to be staging a comeback here, at least to the extent that a systems analysis kind of description involves notions of contributing to, or moving towards, a final goal. However, the great problem was to incorporate, not purpose, but consciousness. Doing without ideas seemed to deny (or at least neglect) consciousness, and this remains true whether we replace them by functional states, behaviour or brain states. If the brain is a computer then it can be given a systems-analysis description without any mention of consciousness. On the other hand, most of us think that we, unlike computers, *are* conscious. And we think this is an important fact about us, something vital to any explanation of why we do the things we do. Functionalism denies this.

Behaviourism, mind/brain identity theories, and functionalism are all forms of *physicalism*, since they claim that we are essentially physical – Descartes, by contrast, claimed that we are essentially mental. Broadly speaking, there are two physicalist responses to our introspective claims to a mental life. The heroic line is just to deny what we seem to experience, to dismiss our claims to consciousness as some sort of illusion. A more temperate response is to accept consciousness, but then subordinate it in some way to the overriding importance of behaviour, brain states or functional states. B. F. Skinner seems to have been a pretty heroic behaviourist: Gilbert Ryle's stylishly behaviourist book *The Concept of Mind* aspires to heroism, and often achieves it, but under severe pressure sometimes retreats into temperance. Richard Rorty's Disappearance Theory and its contemporary Eliminativist successors can be classified as heroic mind/brain identity theories: other identity and double aspect theories can be a bit more temperate.

Now functionalism is not intrinsically cast in the heroic mould. It is committed to denying only the explanatory relevance, not the existence, of consciousness. But then what should a functionalist say about our conviction that the mental events we seem to be conscious of *are* relevant to the things we do and say? Is it possible to say that the stream of consciousness is the series of functional states as 'seen from the inside'? No, because a functional state isn't the sort of thing which can be seen or experienced. But I suppose it is at least *possible* that the stream of consciousness is the series of brain states which implements the series of functional states, as those brain states are experienced by the subject.

The role of the brain

Let's take an example. Talking about the pleasure we derive from listening to music, and indeed about pleasure more generally, Robert Jourdain says, 'the nervous system functions the same way in all its reaches. The same basic

Functionalism in
biology

Present-day biology has
made tremendous progress
on the assumption that
genes code for macroscopic
features. The basic idea has
been that a particular gene
might code for the colour of
a flower, for example, or the
shape of the seed pod.

Recent research suggests,
however, that this coding
metaphor is coming to the
end of its usefulness. 'Gene
knockout' studies show that
features thought to be
produced by particular
genes can still occur, even if
that gene is switched off. We
may therefore have to think
of large networks of
proteins (including many
genes) acting together, rather
than identifying function with
single physical components.
In short, we may well find in
molecular biology too, that a
functionalist account is more
explanatory.

Benedict de Spinoza (1632–1677) on
mind and body:

'. . . people . . . are firmly convinced
that it is by the command of the mind
alone that the body moves at one
time and is at rest at another . . . No
one, however, has yet settled what the
body is capable of . . . considered
simply as something corporeal . . . no
one has yet achieved such an accurate
knowledge of the structure of the
body as to be able to explain all its
functions.

Moreover, no one yet knows in
what way and by what means the
mind moves the body . . . the body
alone, merely from the laws of its
nature, is capable of many things that
astonish the mind . . .

It follows that when men say that
this or that action has its origins in the
mind which has control over the
body, they really do not know what
they are talking about, and are only
dressing up in fancy language their
admission that, apart from being
amazed at the action, they are
ignorant of its true cause.' *Ethics*
(written in the mid-1660s, and every
bit as true today as it was then)

mechanism applies to all pleasures, artistic and otherwise, for the simple reason that this mechanism *is* pleasure' (*Music, the Brain & Ecstasy,* 1998). The view sketched in the last paragraph regards this simple reason as much *too* simple. It says that pleasure has two aspects. The subjective experience – the *feeling* – of pleasure is the experienced aspect of those mechanisms of the nervous system centrally involved in the functional states which constitute the objective aspect of pleasure. These functional states will usually be too complex to list exhaustively, but they will specify *input* states (such as listening to such-and-such a piece of music under conditions of reasonable satiety and relaxation), *processing* states (such as comparing the present performance with remembered ones), and *output* states (such as applauding loudly or buying the CD). Pleasure in its objective aspect – as something useful for explaining behaviour – is a shorthand way of referring to these very numerous and complex functional states.

A standard objection to any view of this kind is that brain states have properties, such as spatial location, which can't be ascribed to mental states. A mental image of Marilyn Monroe, for example, cannot be a brain-state as that brain-state appears to the brain's owner, because the brain-state can – and the mental image cannot – be given a location in space. The relevant brain-state is located somewhere a few centimetres behind the owner's nose: the mental image isn't anywhere. The objection, then, is that the stream of consciousness cannot be identified with any series of brain-states, because these two things have incompatible properties: one has spatial location and the other does not.

But it's by no means clear that all properties have to be cross-applicable in cases of seeing-as or experiencing-as. To adapt an example of Wittgenstein's, I can see a triangle as a mountain or as an arrow (or of course as a triangle). Seen as a mountain it has height: seen as an arrow it points. But neither of these properties makes much sense if cross-applied. Other examples are easily devised. A modern art installation, seen from the side, might look only like a jumble of metal pipes. Seen from the front, it might look like a parody of the Mona Lisa. To the parody, adjectives like 'witty' or 'affectionate' might be appropriate, in spite of making no sense when applied to the jumble.

In Chapter 5 we distinguished between Descartes' substance-dualism (two sorts of stuff in the world) and modern forms of property-dualism (one sort of stuff with two sorts of properties). For property-dualism, incompatible properties would indeed be a stumbling-block. But the idea under consideration here is *aspect*-dualism (if that still deserves the name of dualism). And it's clear that one and the same thing, when seen under different aspects, can have incompatible properties. So perhaps brain-states (experienced from the outside) could have spatial location, while the same brain-states (experienced from the inside) might not.

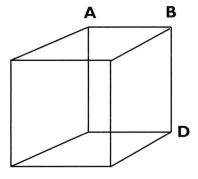

A B
D

We can see the Necker cube as having the corners A, B and D at the front or – incompatibly – at the back.

Aspect-dualism

One advantage of aspect-dualism is that it suggests that the question whether states of consciousness are identical with brain-states is misplaced. Is the ABD-to-the-front aspect of the Necker cube identical with the disposition of ink molecules on the page?

On the other hand, aspect-dualism does not solve the problem of qualia (though perhaps it lets us see what the root of the problem is). Thus, science is essentially *public*. A scientific experiment must be one which other researchers can repeat. A scientific claim must be one which someone else can responsibly make. But the way my brain-states seem to me is a kind of fact which (it seems) no one else could have access to. It's for *this* reason that a scientific account of human kind will leave out qualia. As Nagel said, 'every subjective phenomenon is essentially connected with a single point of view, and it seems inevitable that an objective, physical theory will abandon that point of view'.

The question which follows is: are qualia *real*? Is the 'how-it-seems-to-me' of my brain-states part of the furniture of the universe? And the first step in finding the answer to this vexing question, as we saw in Chapter 4, will be more clarity about what we mean by the word 'real'.

Spinoza may have had something like aspect-dualism in mind when he wrote:

'The mind and the body are one and the same thing, which is conceived now under the attribute of thought, now under the attribute of extension.' *Ethics* (1677)

Another objection is that aspect-dualism implies that whenever we are conscious, what we are conscious of is really our own brain. The object of consciousness is neither the orchid nor the orchid-idea caused by it, but an orchid-brain-state. And now a 'veil of brain-states' seems to descend. If we are only ever conscious of our own brain-states, how do we get beyond them? How do we justify belief in orchids, or anything else out there – especially if any belief, and any evidence produced in its favour, is just another brain-state as it appears 'from the inside'?

We can respond to this objection in two ways. It is possible to argue, first, that although we experience brain-states as the stream of consciousness, that does not imply that we are conscious of brain-states and nothing else. Brain-states might be the sole *occasions* of consciousness without being the sole *objects* of consciousness. Secondly, and more to the point, we should accept that there is a genuine veil-type problem here, and argue that it is a sceptical problem which arises quite generally for anyone who regards the brain as the single channel of inputs to consciousness (as I suppose we all do). It is not uniquely or distinctively a problem for aspect-dualism.

Conclusion

So I would guess that some form of temperate functionalism combined with aspect-dualism might at least be tenable, if we can solve the 'veil of brain-states' problem. Any heroic view seems to me impossible to believe, short of revolutionary changes in our concept of ourselves. This 'aspect-functionalism' would allow us to justify our belief that others have mental states (though we would not experience their mental states from the point of view that they do). It would give mental states a role in explaining action, and although this role would be distant and inessential, it would involve purposive rather than merely correlational causality. It would also place us in the external world as responsive and exploring natural systems, since our brain states are part of the natural world and causally bound up with it. If these advantages are really within our grasp, they would certainly be worth having.

Well, great deeds remain to be done in the philosophy of mind. We haven't explained yet why ideas were so fatally attractive, nor have we calmed all doubts about regarding mental states as brain-states 'seen from the inside'. And the notion of a functional state is so far very vague, perhaps too vague to be scientific, as one of its first exponents, Hilary Putnam, has recently argued. It might be, for example, that a functionalist explanation is not really an alternative, but only a preliminary, to a fully 'atomistic' account. But somehow, a shallow optimism overtakes me when I think about the mind. We *may* be on the verge of making sense.

The Chinese room argument

Could a computer really *understand* what you say to it? Or are the commands you enter just like the key you put into a lock, producing the desired result mechanically?

Suppose you were in a room with a big pile of cards and a rule book. The cards have Chinese characters written on them (we're assuming you don't read Chinese). The rule book lists input-output relations: when such-and-such a sequence of cards comes in, send such-and-such a sequence of cards out. It's clear that, if your rule book was good enough, you could produce coherent responses to incoming Chinese sentences (coherent to someone who does read Chinese) without understanding a single card. In the same way, a computer with a good enough rule-book (i.e. program) could produce coherent, human-like, responses in English, without understanding a single word it 'says'.

This 'Chinese room' argument is due to John Searle, who claims that 'no computer program can ever be a mind'. According to Searle, only the special machines we call brains can think.

The argument, predictably, has not gone down well with those who find a computer model of the mind appealing. But it has the merit, at least, of forcing us to ask again whether human-like output really is — as the famous Turing Test assumes — a sufficient test of understanding.

Do you agree . . . ?

1. **Spinoza was right: to say that behaviour is caused by the mind is just a confession of ignorance.**

2. **To say that behaviour is not caused by the mind requires us to pretend that we are zombies.**

3. **Computers are unlike us in having no consciousness.**

4. **All our knowledge of the world comes to us by way of the brain.**

CHAPTER 22

Truth

We suggested in the last chapter that there might be no ideas, and in the chapter before that, that there might be no independent external world. How, then, should we understand truth? Common sense sees a true belief as one which corresponds to the way things really are, but both sides of this alleged correspondence are now in doubt. In this chapter, we look at the correspondence theory of truth and its rivals.

As we saw in Chapter 20, Locke understood perception in terms of resemblance (or the lack of it) between an inner object and an outer one. Perception is accurate or reliable when the inner object mirrors the outer one, inaccurate or misleading when it doesn't. Our senses tell us the truth about the world when inner corresponds to outer. When the correspondence breaks down, they fib.

Part of the appeal of this account is that it transfers to the topic of perception an ancient and almost irresistible theory of truth, the so-called correspondence theory. Why, you may ask, do we need a theory of truth? Well, perhaps we don't, really. In the twentieth century some philosophers have insisted that we don't *at all* need a theory of truth, and we'll come back to that view in due course. But the question seems so harmless. Surely we know what we mean when we say that something's true. So explain . . .

The irresistible answer is that when we say something true, things *are* as we say they are. If we say the toy soldiers are lined up neatly, and they *are* lined up neatly, why then, what we said is true. The supreme obviousness of this answer tends to suggest that the question is fair enough, if a bit easier than we're used to.

The correspondence theory

But let's go a step further. When we say that things are as they are said to be, what does that mean exactly? Can't we explain in some less roundabout fashion? This seems almost as easy: things are as they are said to be, when the way they are *corresponds to* the way they are said to be. Truth, to put it in a nutshell, can be defined as a correspondence between assertion and reality.

Wonderful. Now, how do we detect this 'correspondence' in any particular case? What makes it true that this particular arrangement of toy soldiers, for example, corresponds to the words 'lined up neatly'? Well, there must be two sides to a correspondence. The words 'lined up neatly' must represent things as forming some recognisable shape, such as a straight line. And when we look at the toy soldiers, we see some such shape. Perhaps the words summon up ideas in our minds, which match the ideas produced by looking at the actual arrangement of toy soldiers.

As Aristotle said:

'To say of what is that it is not, or of what is not that it is, is false, while to say of what is that it is, or of what is not that it is not, is true.'
Metaphysics (date uncertain)

Language 'Corresponding to' Reality

THE
CAT

SAT
ON

THE
MAT

But if correspondence is explained (as above) in terms of ideas, the by-now-familiar veil of appearances problems arise, making correspondence impossible to establish in any real case. And even in a version which does not depend on Lockean ideas, the suggestion is that we first establish a correspondence, and on that basis pronounce the statement true. But how do we establish this correspondence? If we just understand what's been asserted and look at the situation, then talking about 'correspondence' gives us no new handle on truth. We just understand and look. If, on the other hand, correspondence is a mystery relation – unanalysable, *sui generis*, primitive or whatever – that too gives us no new understanding of truth. So it seems that correspondence either commits us to something impossible to discover, or tells us nothing new. And in either case we return empty-handed to our question: what does it mean to say that things are as they are said to be? What can be said in explanation of that little word 'as'?

Coherence and pragmatism

Some people, despairing of correspondence, have tried to explain what we mean by truth in other ways. One view points out that the things we accept as true fit together to form a single system. They *cohere*. Perhaps when we say something is true we just mean that it fits together with everything else we believe. This line has been popular with idealists, who are obviously going to feel a bit unhappy about correspondence with an external world, if there isn't one.

Unfortunately, 'coherence' tends to behave just like 'correspondence' did. Ask how we discover it in any particular case and it tends either to turn into something impossible to establish (like Joachim's 'mystical ideal') or to tell us nothing new about truth after all. If the coherence of two beliefs is explained in terms of logical consistency, for example, it *presupposes* truth rather than explaining it, because to say that two statements are logically consistent is to say that they can both be 'true' at the same time.

So let's move smartly along to pragmatism (currently being revived as a distinctively American theory). On this view, to say that something is true is to say that it works, or makes your life better if you believe it. William James (1842–1910) wrote: 'You can say . . . either that "it is useful because it is true" or that "it is true because it is useful." Both these phrases mean exactly the same thing. Or more bluntly: '"The true", to put it briefly, is only the expedient in the way of our thinking, just as "the right" is only the expedient in the way of our behaving' (*Pragmatism*, 1907).

This seems to imply that it *could not* be true that the sun exploded seven minutes ago, since, far from making life better, the unfortunate result would be the extinction of all life on earth, in about a minute's time. If it is now suggested that 'working' means in this case 'generating successful predictions'

C. S. Peirce

C. S. Peirce (1839–1914) on truth:

'The opinion which is fated to be ultimately agreed to by all who investigate is what we mean by truth and the object represented by this opinion is the real.'

This 'ideal limit' theory of truth is more interesting than its Jamesian contemporary, pragmatism. Unfortunately, it's not without problems of its own.

If we are ever to be able to say that a statement is true, we must, on this account, know that investigation has reached its ultimate point. How could we know this? As before, it seems either that we cannot be sure that the ultimate point has been reached, or that we know it has been reached because we believe the result is true (which means that the ideal limit theory depends on truth rather than explaining it).

Locke ditto:

Locke did his best to get the best of both worlds, distinguishing between 'verbal' truth (the kind of truth which a coherence theory describes) and 'real' truth (secured by correspondence). He writes:

'. . . that being only verbal truth, wherein terms are joined according to the agreement or disagreement of the ideas they stand for; without regarding whether our ideas are such as really have an existence in nature . . . They contain *real truth* when our ideas are such as we know are capable of having an existence in nature.'
Essay (1689)

or 'fitting into the rest of what we know', we seem to have returned to either a correspondence or coherence theory. And the same destinations seem to await us if we ask *why* a true statement or belief has good consequences (if it does). Isn't it because a true statement tells us how things really are, or fits in nicely with everything else we know? In the same way, we can also ask of the coherence theory why it is that exactly *this* set of statements coheres together. Is it a coincidence? The common sense reply is that they cohere because they correspond to a *single* world, and this returns us to the correspondence theory, very much square one for theories of truth.

The redundancy theory

However, an interesting recent theory holds that when we say a statement is true, we are not saying anything as substantial as the correspondence, coherence and pragmatist theories make out. We are not relating the statement to something *else* (whether the external world, our existing body of knowledge, or the future consequences of believing it). We are not making some extra factual claim. Instead, we are declaring our support for the statement, or asserting it in a more emphatic or concessive form. In short, 'is true' has performative, non-factual, meaning.

There's no doubt that we do use 'is true' in these ways, to support and emphasise. But how do we *decide* to support one statement and not another? Why do we want to emphasise a particular statement and concede another? This is not a matter of whim. In fact, we add these extra performative levels of meaning because we think the statement in question tells us how things are, or is required by everything else we believe, or is important for coping successfully with life. So to be interesting, the claim (of this new 'redundancy' theory of truth) must be that our reasons for declaring a statement true are not part of what we *mean* by calling it true. Interpreted in this way, the redundancy theory claims that our original question (about what we mean when we say something is true) is sufficiently answered by listing the performative uses of the expression. Giving a general account of our *reasons* for saying that a statement is true is a different enterprise.

If we accept this, the next question is whether it's worth embarking on this different enterprise. *Should* we try to characterise, in a general way, our reasons for believing a statement to be true, or should we not?

Well it's perfectly possible to say 'Not', and those impressed by Wittgenstein's idea of a family resemblance concept will have been itching to say this for some time. Wittgenstein pointed out that lots of our ordinary everyday ideas don't have any neat definition. Could you define what a chair is, so that there are *no* odd chairs left out, and *no* non-chairs inadvertently brought in? Could you define the word 'game' so that it includes for example rugby and solitaire, along

William James

Frank Ramsey (1903–1930) on truth:

'. . . it is evident that "It is true that Caesar was murdered" means no more than that Caesar was murdered, and "It is false that Caesar was murdered" means that Caesar was not murdered. They are phrases which we sometimes use for emphasis or for stylistic reasons . . .' *Facts and Propositions* (1927)

Performative utterances

The notion of a performative utterance is due to J. L. Austin. A performative utterance looks (at least grammatically) like an assertion which could be true or false, but it is used, not to describe or report, but to perform an action. 'I promise I'll be there' is an example, and so is 'I warn you not to go'.

So, if 'It's true that Caesar was murdered' means the same as 'I accept or concede that Caesar was murdered', and if 'I accept' or 'I concede' is like 'I promise' or 'I warn', then truth is performative.

with bridge, online role-playing, and catch? We can operate with 'chair', 'game' and many other concepts, Wittgenstein thought, not because we have a neat paper definition, but because we have a repertoire of examples.

Wittgenstein meant this as a warning against the common sense idea (from which Socrates got such wonderful mileage) that if we call a lot of things by a single name, then there *must* be something that they all have in common. If Wittgenstein is right, when we call different statements true, there might not be *anything* common to all those statements, or to our decisions to endorse them. Perhaps we have one sort of reason for endorsing mathematical truths, another sort for moral truths, yet another sort of reason for everyday truths about what is going on around us, and still others for the truths of economics or particle physics. If so, the attempt to give a single, general characterisation of our reasons for holding a statement true, is doomed from the start.

Wittgenstein's warning against the search for *essences* is important, but it obviously doesn't mean that all attempts to generalise are doomed. On the contrary, it explains how generalisation works, at least in many cases (that is, by paradigm examples and spontaneous extensions from them, rather than by paper definition). What we ought to do is therefore to give paradigm examples of truth – and this, thank goodness, is simplicity itself. The toy soldiers example will do for one, and I'm sure anyone can supply a hundred more.

Conclusion

So what went wrong before? We said that the statement 'The toy soldiers are lined up neatly' is true if the toy soldiers are . . . well . . . lined up neatly. As an account of what it means to say that a statement is true, this seemed less than explanatory, and so we were tempted to introduce a big word ('correspondence' or 'coherence' or the rest) in the hope that one of them would paper over the explanatory crack. But as soon as we asked for an account of 'correspondence' etc., the explanatory promise of the big words evaporated, leaving only paradox and mystery.

You may recall that in Chapter 17 we gave up the attempt to provide a definition of resemblance on the grounds that resemblance is too basic to be explained in terms of any other concept. We decided to supply examples on demand, but not a definition. Well, the same thing has just happened with truth. This time, however, what might have looked like simple failure (to find the definition we were looking for) can be explained by Wittgenstein's insight that concept-formation frequently, and properly, works by examples not definitions. This allows us to accept the almost irresistible correspondence theory, as long as we explain what 'correspondence' means by giving examples – resisting the lure of the paper definition.

There now. Who says you never get anywhere in philosophy?

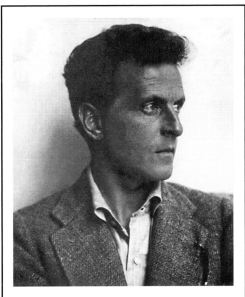

Ludwig Wittgenstein

Wittgenstein on how we classify:

'How should we explain to someone what a game is? I imagine that we should describe *games* to him, and we might add: "This *and similar things* are called 'games'"'. And do we know any more about it ourselves? Is it only other people whom we cannot tell exactly what a game is?' *Philosophical Investigations* (1953)

Notice that the claim that we classify by examples and spontaneous extension, goes well beyond the claim that we classify by multiple not single resemblances (see Chapter 16).

Do you agree . . . ?

1. **A statement is true if it corresponds to the facts.**

    _____

2. **A statement is true if believing it makes you happier than not believing it.**

    _____

3. **A concept like 'truth' cannot be given a paper definition.**

    _____

4. **We all understand what we mean by 'true' so there's no need to give a definition.**

    _____

CHAPTER 23

Objectivity

The last chapter defended an 'unpretentious' correspondence theory of truth. We now return to the issue of the independence of reality, in order to unify many of the problems we have considered (as problems of 'anti-realism').

So our reasons for accepting a statement as true *do* generalise, and we can give the generalisation: true statements correspond to reality. What's more, asserting this generalisation might be important, for example at the birth of a new science (as in the controversy surrounding E. A. Milne in the thirties, about relativistic cosmology). But *explaining* the generalisation is a matter of providing paradigm examples, not paper definitions. Or to put it another way, correspondence is an alternative *idiom for*, not an ultimate *explanation of*, truth.

Well, that probably seems too easy – and so it is. For one thing, it leaves the urge to find an explanation of truth unresolved. And I'm afraid there's another big fish, close kin to the problem of defining truth, lurking beneath the waves. The name of this monster is Objectivity.

A statement is objective, we fondly suppose, if it's made true by the way things are, *independently of us*. Here we have a kind of beefed-up correspondence (between what we say and the way things are), now being employed to explain a more objective, that is, more rigorous, or more scientific, or 'perspective-less', or at any rate *better* kind of truth. 'The toy soldiers are lined up neatly' is true if they really are lined up neatly, but it's not *objectively* true because 'neatly' is not observer-independent. There's an element of subjective opinion here.

'Independent facts'

This evaluative element is one way in which a statement might fall short of objectivity, but of course there are lots of others. Someone might argue that 'soldier' is not objective either, because differences of opinion are possible about whether a given individual is a soldier or a freedom fighter, prison guard, terrorist, armed policeman, spy etc. In the same way, it might be argued that 'lined up' depends on a human propensity for seeing patterns, when all that's really present is one individual, then another, then another. And the word 'toy' obviously depends on the cultural practice of giving children things

The 'failure' of correspondence

Berkeley reacted to Locke's claimed correspondence between the inner and the outer world by arguing that if the two can't be independently accessed, there might as well be only one. And it's tempting to react to the perceived failure of the correspondence theory of truth in the same rigorous spirit, arguing that if we can't define what correspondence between language and reality might be, then that distinction too is a sham – there's only language, all the way down. Richard Rorty (1931–) supports one version of this view:

'... the Derridean claim that "There is nothing outside the text" is right about what it implicitly denies and wrong about what it explicitly asserts. The only force of saying that texts do not refer to non-texts is just the old pragmatist chestnut that any specification of a referent is going to be in some vocabulary. Thus one is comparing two descriptions of a thing rather than a description with the thing-in-itself. This chestnut ... [is] a restatement of Berkeley's ingenuous remark "nothing can be like an idea except an idea". These are all merely misleading ways of saying that we shall not see reality plain, unmasked, naked to our gaze.' *Consequences of Pragmatism* (1982)

Do you remember that image of nature's face completely covered by the mask of theory (way back in Chapter 1)? If the mask really *cannot* be removed, the supposition that there's a face underneath is surplus to requirements.

to play with. In the final list of Contents of the Universe, there are no *toys*. And so on.

Among these various senses of 'objective' one which seems particularly interesting is independence of human language. In this sense, to say that things are objectively thus-and-so is to say that their being thus-and-so does not depend on how we choose to describe or classify them. The contrary view (argued, up to a point, by Sapir and Whorf) is that language constructs reality – there is no fact of the matter about how things are, independently of how we describe them in words. Well, there *are* important problems about 'factoring out' our own preferences, language, culture and psychology in order to achieve a more objective kind of knowledge. But I want to sidestep these fashionable problems of relativism and concentrate instead on the more general idea that things are independent of our *knowledge* of them. To say that things are observer-independent, in this sense, is to say that they are in whatever state they're in, whether we know about it or not. The world is the way it is, quite irrespective of what we happen to have found out about it.

This seems like common sense. After all, the earth was presumably in a particular, quite definite state, before any sentient life existed to take any kind of notice of it. And when, by the Law of Entropy, the entire universe has turned into a thin mist of freezing, undifferentiated gas, it will presumably *be* freezing, undifferentiated gas, even though no intelligent life will be around to bear witness to the fact. In short, common sense (and science too, some of the time) works with a concept of objective or knowledge-independent reality. We might say, for the sake of a label, that common sense is objectivist about the world.

Common sense is also objectivist about other people's mental lives. We normally believe that other people have a mental life like ours, which does not depend on the state of any observer's knowledge of it. Marion's daydream is what it is, regardless of what you or I may know about it.

Common sense is also objectivist about the past. We normally think that facts about the remote past are perfectly definite, though nobody now does, ever did, or perhaps ever will, know them. How could the past have brought about the present if it wasn't as real as the present? And how could the present cognitive state, of one particular species, on one little planet, make a difference to the reality of the past?

Problems for independence

But suppose that the allegedly 'independent' state of affairs is not something we happen not to know about, but could find out about if we wanted to. Suppose, as seems to be systematically the case, it's something we *can't* find

Relativism

'Relativism' must have a strong claim to be the most unhelpful word in philosophy. Not only has it no agreed meaning, it somehow creates strong emotional reactions, either for or against.

Still, there's an important cluster of issues here (which is why the word keeps coming up), so it's probably worth trying to say what the main different kinds of relativism are. Here goes . . .

A relativist first divides people into insiders and outsiders, depending on participation in some set of beliefs and practices. The relativist then focuses on either the *value*, or the *meaning*, or the *rationality*, or the *truth*, of this set, and claims (in order of increasing toxicity):

1. that any assessment by outsiders involves participation in some similar or competing set of beliefs and practices, and/or
2. that it's OK for insiders and outsiders to assess the beliefs and practices differently, and/or
3. that outsiders cannot properly assess them at all.

So for example, a type-1 relativist about *truth* might claim that there is no God's-eye view from which we can see how things really are. A type-2 relativist about *value* might claim that it's OK for different people to say very different things about the value of believing in God, or the value of abstract painting, or the value of compassion. The apparent disagreement is not one we should expect or try to resolve. A type-3 relativist about *meaning* might claim, for example, that Western (or Eastern) anthropologists cannot say what Azande beliefs about magic really mean to the Azande.

A view sometimes attributed to Wittgenstein is that criteria for rationality only exist within a large-scale practice (such as Western medicine or Azande magic): there are no criteria for the rationality of the practice as a whole. According to the above framework, this view would not count as a form of relativism, since it says that questions of rationality directed at the practice as a whole cannot be answered (or for that matter asked) even by insiders.

The framework distinguishes twelve main types of relativism in all, some of them eminently plausible, some pretty wild. But a taxonomy of this kind only maps the battlefield. The hard work of resolving the underlying tension between individual freedom and objective standards – somehow or other – lies before us.

out about. Common sense also holds that we cannot find out (in any direct way) about other people's mental lives. We can only find out indirectly, by observing or asking them. Similarly, we can't find out (in any direct way) about the remote past. We can only make inferences from present or future evidence. And given the problems we've seen with perception, it seems we can't find out directly about the external world either. We have to infer how things really are, from our experiences.

What's more, even if this does not apply at the macroscopic level, as the result of a mentalistic analysis of perception, our best current science seems to tell us that it does apply at the sub-atomic level, as the result of the impact of the act of measuring on the 'thing' measured (see the end of Chapter 20).

In all these cases, then, our old problems rise again: how can there be indirect knowledge when there cannot possibly be direct knowledge? And if all our concepts come to us through experience (as empiricism claims), how can we even have a concept of things we've never directly experienced and don't know anything about? The first question attacks our claim to know, the second our claim to understand anything at all about other minds, the past, the external world (and a number of other things I haven't mentioned). The first question is a form of scepticism, the second a form of 'anti-realism' – so called because it holds that the idea of a *reality* independent of human knowledge makes no sense.

What's happening here is that, under pressure from the difficulties raised for 'direct' knowledge, common sense gives up the claim to 'directness'. It refuses, however, to give up the claim that the objects of knowledge are 'independent'. It insists that even if our knowledge is inevitably mediated by our sensory equipment or our procedures for finding out, still, the thing we gain knowledge *of* is independent of that equipment and those procedures. But what's the point of insisting that things are independent if they only ever come to us in dependent form?

A defence of common sense

One interesting way of defending common sense is to say that 'direct' and 'independent' (like other family resemblance concepts) get their meaning from a repertoire of examples. The paradigm case of direct perception is, let's say, seeing something medium-sized and stationary, at an appropriate distance and in good light. An apple at arm's length on a sunny day, for example. This is also a paradigm case of an independent thing: the apple doesn't change whether I look at it or look away.

When it's pointed out that there are all sorts of complex optical and neural processes between the apple and my seeing of it, common sense reluctantly

Michael Dummett (1925–) writes:

'Realism I characterise as the belief that statements of the disputed class [e.g. statements about the external world, mental events, mathematical entities, the past or future etc.] possess an objective truth-value, independently of our means of knowing it: they are true or false in virtue of a reality existing independently of us.' *Truth and Other Enigmas* (1978)

Anti-realism does not say that reality depends on human knowledge, or that all properties are 'interactional' (see Chapter 20), or that the external world does not exist (these being forms of Idealism). It says that we cannot talk meaningfully about anything we cannot possibly know. We cannot for example *assert* the existence of an unknowable reality – and we can't *deny* it either. The anti-realist's slogan is: whereof we cannot know, thereof we cannot speak.

concedes that if all those processes come between, the relation can't be direct. Common sense gives up the claim that this is a case of 'direct' perception. But perhaps that's a mistake. After all, what could be *more* direct than the 'apple on a sunny day' kind of case? If *this* isn't direct knowledge of an independent entity, the words 'direct' and 'independent' lose their meaning (because this is the kind of example which fixes their meaning). But if 'direct' and 'independent' lose their meaning, then 'dependent' or 'indirect' lose their meaning too, and no longer signal anything inferior in things or our knowledge of them. Common sense, according to this attempted defence of it, should therefore stoutly insist on its claims to directness and independence, since the challenges to them depend on an unnoticed change in the meanings given to the words.

My own opinion is that even if this dangerous argument succeeds, the 'veil' problems (of appearances or brain-states) will still require attention. But rather than pursue that now, I'd like you to cast your mind back to Berkeley's appeal to God. According to Berkeley, God perceives all those essential bits and pieces which nobody else is keeping an eye on, and so guarantees their continued existence independently of us. To anyone of an agnostic turn of mind, and perhaps to a believer too, there is something a little too convenient about this manoeuvre. But Berkeley might be right, after all, to regard God as necessary for the independent existence of the world, at least in the sense that our *notion* of independence of human knowledge (and language, culture, psychology, preference, and what-have-you), depends on our notion of the world as it would appear to an omniscient God.

A need for God?

God is of course supremely independent of everything else, but in addition, His knowledge is not mediated, as ours is, by sensory organs, or by limited and limiting procedures for finding out. As Peter Abelard said, '. . . sense is no impediment to Him who alone has only true understanding'. God stands as the perfect exemplar of both independent existence and direct knowledge.

The question arises, therefore, whether it's possible for a non-believer to have a notion (which common sense appears to need) of the way things are, independently of human knowledge. If human knowledge is always mediated, and if mediated implies dependent, then perhaps only God can provide the inspiration for direct knowledge of an independent reality. Give up on belief in God, it might be argued in transcendental style, and the objective world's a goner too.

We have managed here to unify various problems as problems where our knowledge, though not direct, is nevertheless supposed to be of a knowledge-

independent reality. The common form of the problems is: how can we claim to know, or to talk meaningfully about, a knowledge-independent reality, if it only ever comes to us in dependent (that is, mediated) form? But we can unify the problems further, because the forms of mediation (through the ideas given in perception, through present and future evidence, through other people's observable behaviour, through the readings on our instruments etc.) are all *effects*. All our knowledge of the world, in other words, is in all these cases mediated by some sort of causal process between the thing we claim to know and our knowledge of it. There is always a 'veil of *causes*' between us and it.

Hume said, 'Our reason must be consider'd as a kind of cause, of which truth is the natural effect'. Now, if we could say, independently of its effects, that the *purpose* of our cognitive apparatus is to capture truth (a purpose it has perhaps evolved to carry out), there might be hope. But if the claim is only for correlations, it seems that we would have to have access to the object of our knowledge *not* by means of any of its effects. Otherwise the 'veil of causes' is impenetrable. But this is possible only for a being capable of miraculous (that is, non-causal) knowledge and action. Once again, only God can serve as the inspiration for direct knowledge of an independent reality.

(I ought to point out that there *is* a response to the veil of causes problem, which doesn't appeal to the idea of God. We could try to collapse the gap between the thing we claim to know and its effects. If a thing just *is* its effects, then there's no problem about knowing it *by means of* its effects – except that we might want to stop talking about 'it' and its 'effects' and just talk instead about 'changes'. As a matter of fact, this same reductionist move – so-called because it 'reduces' something problematic to something more directly accessible – is encouraged by the Platonic concept of reality introduced in Chapter 4. We simply move from defining a thing as real if it *has* effects, to saying that its reality *consists* in its effects.

But how could there be effects without 'things' which suffer them? How could there be changes without 'things' which undergo them? We might be able to cope with contactless influence – but can we really make sense of thingless change?)

Waismann on language and reality:

Friedrich Waismann (1896–1959) makes an interesting comparison between colour and lustre. In English, colour is expressed by adjectives, and accordingly, we think of colours as stable properties of things. Lustre, on the other hand, is expressed by verbs (glow, glitter, shine, sparkle and so on). We normally think of lustre as something a thing happens to be doing at a particular moment.

Waismann points out that several languages, including Russian, German and Italian, express colour by means of verbs, and claims that speakers of these languages see colour quite differently. He says, 'The sky which "blues" is seen as something which continually brings forth blueness – it radiates blueness, so to speak; blue does not inhere in it as a mere quality.'

He then imagines a language in which colour is expressed by adverbs applied to verbs of lustre. In this language, one would say, 'The evening clouds glow redly' and so on. According to Waismann, 'the users of such a language would find it very hard to see colour as a quality of things . . . they would see the world with different eyes'.

Examples of this kind, Waismann suggests, undermine the idea of an objective reality which language merely – neutrally – describes.

Do you agree . . . ?

1. Objective truth is better than anything subjective.

_____

2. It is impossible to express facts in language without distorting them.

_____

3. There are facts which nobody will ever know.

_____

4. Only the notion of a God can give substance to our belief in an independent reality.

_____

CHAPTER 24

God

> This chapter discusses one traditional, bewitching and still controversial argument for the existence of God. Apart from its intrinsic interest, the argument will provide a very clear example of the interconnectedness of philosophical problems.

God has had a profound, and arguably beneficial, influence on western philosophy. We have already seen God as Cartesian guarantor of human knowledge, and as threat (through divine foreknowledge) to human freedom. He might also be indispensable (it has just been suggested) as a role-model for perspective-less knowledge of an independent world. But God has also played an important part in our thinking about various other topics, such as infinity, moral and political obligation, and our place in the physical universe as a whole. For all these reasons, philosophers have been intimately involved with God for a long time, and of course, one crucial area of this involvement concerns God's existence. Does He, or doesn't he?

A proof that God exists

In fact, it's quite easy to construct a valid proof that God exists – once you've had the basic, wonderful, idea. An eleventh-century Italian called Anselm (1033–1109), who became Archbishop of Canterbury in 1093, did it in a book called *Proslogion*. His proof goes like this:
1. We understand God as that than which nothing greater can be conceived.
2. If God exists only in our understanding, then something greater than God can be conceived (namely, God existing not only in our understanding but in reality too), but by 1, this is impossible.
3. So God exists not only in our understanding but in reality too.

This ontological argument (as it's called) can be re-phrased in several ways. Here's an alternative formulation which might strike you as simpler:
1. God is the greatest possible being.
2. If we imagine comparing God-not-existing with God-existing, the first is plainly not as great as the second.
3. In order to be the greatest possible being, therefore, God must exist.

As Descartes said in the fifth meditation, 'It is just as much of a contradiction to think of God (that is, a supremely perfect being) lacking existence (that is, lacking a perfection), as it is to think of a mountain without a valley'.

Anselm's proof:

'. . . even the fool [who said in his heart "There is no God"] must agree that there exists, in the understanding at least, something than which nothing greater can be thought; for when he hears this expression he understands it; and whatever is understood exists in the understanding. Yet surely *that than which nothing greater can be thought* cannot exist in the understanding alone. For once granted that it exists, if only in the understanding, it can be thought of as existing in reality, and this is greater. Hence if *that than which a greater cannot be thought* exists solely in the understanding, it would follow that the very thing than which a greater *cannot* be thought turns out to be that than which something greater *can* be thought; but this is clearly impossible. Hence something than which a greater cannot be thought undoubtedly exists both in the understanding and in reality.' *Proslogion* (c.1075)

Both forms of the argument are perfectly valid, and the only question is whether the premisses are true. One popular objection, usually associated with Kant but anticipated by Hume, is that existence is not a perfection. The second premiss in both versions given above asserts that God would be better ('greater') *with* real existence than without it. But, the objection goes, saying that something really exists does not add anything to its description. Unlike 'God is wise, merciful, all-powerful, omniscient etc.' it merely says 'God is'. So while a wise being is greater than a foolish one, the same comparison cannot be run with 'real' in place of 'wise'.

Well, what are we saying when we say something exists or is real? Back in Chapter 4, we thought we were saying that the thing in question has a causal role. Now, having a causal role might be relational rather than intrinsic (that is, might depend on the thing's relations with other things, rather than being a property it has independently of other things). But as we also saw, in Chapter 20, even 'secondary' qualities like colour might well be relational rather than intrinsic. And 'wise', 'powerful', 'merciful', 'omniscient' all certainly involve relations to other things. So it's hard to see why comparisons could not be run as readily with 'existence' as with any of these other properties. And suppose it was argued that, whenever we make a plan, we're implicitly comparing something which does not (yet) exist with the present (existing) state of affairs?

It might be said in reply that having a causal role is more *general* than, for example, having the causal property of tending to make human beings see green. Since it's a matter of having any causal property at all, rather than some specific causal property, existence is not a feature or characteristic of the thing in question. And since it's not a feature or characteristic, we can't add or subtract it like other features for purposes of comparison.

I'm inclined to concede the premiss here and resist the conclusion, that is, to agree that existence is not a property *like* other properties, but insist that the generality of 'having some causal role or other' does not make comparison impossible. If our idea of greatness includes shaping the destiny of nations, appearing in majesty, creating the starry firmament above and all the rest of it, surely we can say that something which does all that is greater than something which doesn't.

There's another route to the same conclusion, and though it involves a slight technicality, it's worth following because it will lead us to what *I* think might be wrong – or if not wrong, problematic – about the ontological argument.

Necessary truth

The technicality is the idea of necessary truth. There are some statements which, though true, could have been false. It's presently true that I'm listening

Anselm

Gottfried Leibniz (1646–1716) on necessary truth:

'There are two kinds of truths: truths of *reasoning* and truths of *fact*. Truths of *reasoning* are necessary and their opposite is impossible; those of *fact* are contingent and their opposite is possible.'
Monadology (1714)

to Mozart, but I *might* have decided to listen to Art Tatum instead. It's true that Krakatoa blew up in 1883, but it *could* have exploded a year earlier or later, or not at all. On the other hand, there are statements which are not just true, but which (we are inclined to say) could not have been false. 'All bachelors are unmarried' seems different in this way from 'All bachelors are untidy'. '2+2 = 4' seems different in the same way from 'Add two drops of water to another two drops, and you'll end up with four drops'. 'Is the Pope a Catholic?' is a rhetorical question, and by contrast 'Is the Prime Minister a Catholic?' is a genuine question, because of this same contrast.

It won't surprise you to learn that we don't have any agreed account of this difference. Still, there does seem to be some sort of difference, and its relevance to the ontological argument is simply that 'God exists' seems to belong on the necessary side of whatever distinction we have here. So we can formulate another version of the argument, like this:

1. 'God exists is necessarily true (that is, it's true in the same sort of way as 'All bachelors are unmarried', and '2+2=4', and 'The Pope is a Catholic').
2. Whatever is asserted in a necessary truth must obtain in the real world.
3. God exists.

The popular objection we were discussing a moment ago now urges, against premiss 1, that 'God exists' can't be a necessary truth: it says that all truths about existence (that is, about causal relations) are contingent. I know this doesn't look like the same objection, but for Kant it's the same because Kant supposed that the predicate of a necessary truth tells us something about the subject, something which is already included in the idea of the subject. So if existence is not a predicate, it can't be used to form a necessary truth. For Hume it's the same because Hume thinks necessary truths tell us about the relations between ideas, and since existence is not an idea, again, there cannot be necessary truths about existence.

So the popular objection, in this new guise, says that whatever exists, or participates in causal relations, might not have done. But why shouldn't some truths about existence be necessary? 'There is a solution to the equation "x+2=4"' seems to be a candidate, as does Descartes' 'There is a thought'. And 'There is a habitable planet in the universe' is at least guaranteed by its assertion, as is 'There is an intelligible sentence'. At any rate, we need some better reason than any which has been provided to accept that all truths about existence are contingent.

Necessary truth and correspondence

Paradoxical as it will seem, I think the problem lies in premiss 2, not 1. Do you remember Kant's distinction between noumena (things in themselves) and

Kant on analytic and synthetic:

'Either the predicate B belongs to the subject A, as somewhat which is contained (though covertly) in the conception A; or the predicate B lies completely out of the conception A, although it stands in connection with it. In the first instance, I term the judgement analytical, in the second, synthetical . . . the former adds in the predicate nothing to the conception of the subject, but only analyses it into its constituent conceptions, which were thought already in the subject, although in a confused manner; the latter adds to our conceptions of the subject a predicate which was not contained in it.' *Critique of Pure Reason* (1781)

Hume on necessary existence:

'. . . the idea of existence is nothing different from the idea of any object . . . when after the simple conception of anything we would conceive it as existent, we in reality make no addition to or alteration on our first idea . . . When I think of God, when I think of Him as existent, and when I believe Him to be existent, my idea of Him neither increases nor diminishes.' *Treatise* (1739)

Wittgenstein on rules and propositions which *must* be true:

'. . . there is no sharp boundary between methodological propositions and propositions within a method.
   But wouldn't one have to say then, that there is no sharp boundary between propositions of logic and empirical propositions? The lack of sharpness *is* that of the boundary between *rule* and empirical proposition.' *On Certainty* (1969)

phenomena (things as they seem to us)? This distinction creates scope for a kind of statement which is (transcendentally) necessarily true, but which nevertheless might be false of things in themselves. We cannot deny, for example, that space and time exist. We cannot even conceive this to be false. And yet in the realm of noumena, it might *be* false.

Without committing ourselves to Kant's distinction, we might try out the idea that necessary truths are ones which we could not conceive to be false, but which might in fact *be* false. They are, as it were, things we have to say, not things which must be so. We cannot of course *say* that they might not be so, but when all's said and done, they might not *be* so. There, I said it.

You probably think that's nonsense. Saying it and at the same time not saying it – that's not paradox, it's nonsense. Then what's the opposite view, expressed in premiss 2 above ('Whatever is asserted in a necessary truth must obtain in the real world')? Isn't 2 saying, 'We have to say it, and in addition, it must be so'? But if it's nonsense to *deny* this 'must be so' bit (as I just tried to do), why isn't it nonsense to *assert* it?

In short, perhaps the distinction between 'what we say' and 'how things are' – which works splendidly when what we say might be true or might be false – fails to apply when what we say *has* to be true, or *has* to be false. This might be expected if, for example, necessary truths are really *rules*, not assertions at all (though this idea has problems of its own). It would also follow if Locke was right to suggest (on page 173) that 'verbal truth' is a matter of coherence, while 'real truth' is a matter of correspondence.

Conclusion

What we've seen here is that Anselm's dazzling ontological argument, though it seems to be relevant only to religious belief, in fact forces us to confront hard questions about the status of maths and logic. We seem compelled either to say (following Hume and Kant) that no statements about existence are necessary, or that necessary statements, if they can be true at all, at any rate aren't true because they correspond with the way things are. The alternative is to accept that we can prove, merely from the existence of the *idea* of God, the real existence *of God*.

This seems to me a nice example of the interconnectedness of problems in philosophy. We start out trying simply to establish whether God exists, and before we know where we are, we find ourselves caught up in quite different questions about maths and logic. Most of our illustrations of interconnectedness have centred on the theme of causality, but the fact is, it happens everywhere. As if the questions were not hard enough taken one by one, we seem to be required, in addition, to answer all of them at once.

Guanilo's perfect island

A monk called Guanilo objected against Anselm's proof that it would work just as well for a perfect island. A perfect island which exists only in the imagination isn't perfect, since it would be better if it really existed. So if we can merely form the concept 'a perfect island', a perfect island must exist (which is of course absurd).

Perhaps the best short answer we can extract from Anselm's lengthy reply to Guanilo is that 'perfect' here can only mean 'better than all which exist'. If this is correct, it follows that a perfect island might not actually exist, making up for this solitary defect by its other, imagined, excellences. Thus, something which does not exist, Anselm says, might be perfect (that is, greater than anything actually existing), but it could not be greater than anything conceivable. Only God has to be defined in terms of the inconceivability of anything greater.

Anselm concludes: 'I believe I have shown . . . by an argument that is not weak but necessary enough, that I did prove the actual existence of a thing than which nothing greater can be conceived.'

Do you agree . . . ?

1. **The ontological argument proves that God exists.**

_____

2. **It's impossible to compare something which exists with something which doesn't.**

_____

3. **Necessary truths do not state facts about the world but rules for the use of words.**

_____

CHAPTER 25

Cause and Design

In this chapter, we look at two further arguments intended to prove that God exists. One turns on the claim that God gives the universe the purpose we can see in it. The other urges that God is the first cause of all the changes we see around us.

There are other arguments for God's existence besides Anselm's ontological argument. And since the running theme of this little book has been the continuing tension between causes and purposes, it's nice that we can end with a topic where the two are divinely reconciled.

Design first. When we look around us, we see many striking examples of well-adaptedness. Indeed, the more we get to know about the world, the more striking and more numerous these examples become. One favourite illustration has been the human eye, a complex arrangement of different kinds of tissue, performing all the different functions necessary to focus light onto a light-sensitive array. Without a clear lens, no light would reach the array: without the array, the light would not be converted into signals the brain can deal with. So these separate elements of the eye need each other in order to function. Useless in themselves, when assembled, they bring forth wonders.

One can understand something growing to fit the space available, or to take some predetermined shape. But this *coordination* of individually useless parts looks very like human foresight and planning – as when a watch-maker assembles something which keeps time, from a pile of intricate pieces, none of which, individually, is much use for anything at all. Even Hume seems to have accepted (in his important *Dialogues Concerning Natural Religion*) that we can infer, cautiously, from similar effects to similar causes, and given his account of causality he could hardly do otherwise. So, if the parts of the eye are like the parts of a watch (in respect of coordination for a function they could not achieve alone), then perhaps there is something *like* human intelligence behind the marvels of adaptation.

Natural selection

This argument took a severe knock in 1859, when Darwin (1809–1882) published *The Origin of Species by Means of Natural Selection*. If a better eye will help an animal survive longer and produce more offspring, and if these offspring will tend to inherit the same improved eye themselves (in spite of the random variations which accidentally produced their parent's superior eye),

Joseph Priestley (1733–1804), semi-discoverer of oxygen, wrote:

'Will any person say that an eye could have been constructed by a being who had no knowledge of optics, who did not know the nature of light, or the laws of refraction? . . . there must be some uncaused intelligent being, the original and designing cause of all other beings.' *Letters to a Philosophical Unbeliever* (1780)

One of the characters in Hume's *Dialogues* puts it like this:

'The curious adapting of means to ends, throughout all nature, resembles exactly, though it much exceeds, the productions of human contrivance – of human design, thought, wisdom and intelligence. Since, therefore the effects resemble each other, we are led to infer, by all the rules of analogy, that the causes also resemble, and that the Author of nature is somewhat similar to the mind of man, though possessed of much larger faculties, proportioned to the grandeur of the work which he has executed.' *Dialogues* (1779)

And Hume himself says:

'A purpose, an intention, a design is evident in every thing; and when our comprehension is so far enlarged as to contemplate the first rise of this visible system, we must adopt, with the strongest conviction, the idea of some intelligent cause or author.' *Natural History of Religion* (1757)

then given a sufficient number of generations, improvements in the eye, and in everything else, will happen naturally. We will end up with something which *looks* designed, because all the changes which didn't work have been eaten.

Biological examples of apparent design can now be explained, therefore, without recourse to 'that hypothesis'. But there's a rather similar argument, beginning from the appearance of *protection*, not design. People sometimes stress how very fortunate it is that our planet is of such-and-such a mass, endowed with water, central heating and an atmosphere, at such-and-such a distance from such-and-such a type of star, and so on. A relatively small change in any of these circumstances, or in the operations of certain crucial laws, and we would all perish. Doesn't it look, therefore, as if a benevolent care-taker had created or reserved this environment just for us? The more we learn about the immensity of space, the more impressed we should be – should we not? – by how very unfriendly most of it is. But the more special our own little corner looks, the more necessary it becomes to explain this specialness. Anything 'special' cries out for explanation. And so the more tempting it becomes to hypothesise something *like* a benevolent human care-taker.

This seems to retreat from the marvels of biology to those of physics or astronomy, but in fact it does nothing of the kind. The important point, the thing to be explained, is the suitability of a certain astronomical and physical environment *for us*. But natural selection provides at least a plausible explanation of this too: the suitability of our environment for us arises from our having adapted to it, not from its having been adapted for us.

Friendliness to life

There's a comeback to this, however. Our particular physiology may have evolved to fit this particular environment, and for this reason its suitability for us may not be providential after all. But why is the earth suitable for any kind of life at all? Lots of other environments (like the moon) cannot support life. So earth remains special, not in being hospitable to *us* in particular, but in being hospitable to life in any shape or form.

Well, it's hard to say just how special this really is, and so it's hard to say exactly how unpalatable the 'brute fact' move is ('It's just a brute fact that the necessary circumstances for life were all in place on this particular planet'). But the longer we go without finding little green men, the more special earth will look, and the more unpalatable the 'brute fact' non-explanation will be.

This argument is often run, not comparing earth with other planets, but comparing the actual universe with all the other possible universes there might have been instead. If the force of gravity, for example, was only one-millionth stronger than it is, no star would survive long enough to permit the evolution of intelligent life. But if hostile possibilities seriously outnumber life-friendly ones,

The evolution of the eye

First, a simple organism acquires, by random mutation, a photo-sensitive area connected with its means of movement or growth. This allows it to react differently to light and dark, which is A Good Thing. As a result, it lives longer and produces more offspring, some of which have the same mutation.

There are now three main processes by which this stroke of good luck is improved upon. Some of the mutated animals acquire, by further mutation, two or more photo-sensitive patches side by side. Others acquire a photo-sensitive patch on some moveable part of the surface. Both accidents allow these animals to react differently to *moving* light, and to light or dark increasing in size. So advantaged, they prosper and leave more offspring than their less fortunate contemporaries.

The third kind of improvement accidentally locates the photo-sensitive patch(es) in a *sunken* area of the body surface, or in an area with a raised edge. This narrows the angle from which light illuminates the photo-receptor(s) and so locates the source more precisely.

Continue these processes of gradual improvement for long enough and we end up with basically three types of advanced eye – the ocellus or eye-cup (multiple photo-receptors all sunken), the compound eye (multiple eye-cups with lenses, in a large array), and the true camera eye (multiple photo-receptors all sunken, with a lens, and moveable).

Life – but not as we know it

Is a candle flame alive? It moves in response to its surroundings. It has definite boundaries, which it maintains over time by eating oxygen and wax, and excreting carbon dioxide and water. In the right conditions it will propagate its kind.

Would an intelligent robot or android be alive? We can suppose that it does not reproduce, or contain code for reproduction. But it sets goals for itself and weighs priorities It can engage in interesting dialogue with us.

In fact, there's no agreed definition of life. Perhaps it's another case where we classify by paradigm examples and spontaneous (which means improvised not undiscussable) extension.

it can be argued that the actual universe (which is obviously at least a *bit* friendly to life) is very unlikely. Therefore requiring explanation, and so on as above.

This version of the argument seems a little weaker in that it requires us to compare possible universes rather than real local environments, but frankly, I don't see a conclusive criticism of either. The crux, I suppose, lies in the principle that similar effects permit us to infer to similar causes. It might well be suggested that we have no grasp of similarity sufficiently clear to get this principle to do any real work for us, and the main importance of Hume's *Dialogues* is, correspondingly, its exploration of rival concepts of similarity. But 'no grasp sufficiently clear' is such a very common complaint that it hardly knocks an argument down.

The first cause argument

On to causes (one last time). If *every* event has a cause, then there is no starting point for the ongoing chain of causes. Any event we tried to regard as the starting-point would have prior causes, and so could not be the real starting-point. But without a starting-point, the chain literally couldn't have got started. Since it evidently has, there must be at least one event which did not require a cause. This event is, obviously, rather special and so particularly demands explanation. Since it can only be likened, in its spontaneity, to our own free acts of the mind, we must (cautiously) suppose that there is something *like* a human mind responsible for beginning the tumult of causes and effects we see around us.

Here's a modern response to this ancient argument (from the cosmologist Jonathan Halliwell):

> 'How did the universe actually begin?' The response of quantum cosmologists to this question may be something of a disappointment. Rather than answer the question, we would declare the question disqualified. In the neighborhood of singularities, such as the initial singularity, the wave functions given by the tunneling and no-boundary proposals indicate that classical general relativity is not valid and, furthermore, that notions of time and space are inappropriate. We cannot, therefore, ask questions involving notions of time or space. (*Scientific American*, 1991)

Halliwell goes on to talk frankly about 'the severe problems of actually testing quantum cosmology observationally', but claims that 'through quantum cosmology we have at least been able to formulate and address the question in a meaningful way'.

Einstein (1879–1955) and others on design:

In his book *The World As I See It* (1949), Einstein had this to say about design in the physical universe:

'[natural law] reveals an intelligence of such superiority that, compared with it, all the systematic thinking and acting of human beings is . . . utterly insignificant'.

The astronomer Sir Fred Hoyle takes the same view:

'. . . a commonsense interpretation of the facts suggests that a superintellect has monkeyed with physics . . . and that there are no blind forces worth speaking about in nature'.

And in the same tradition we find Paul Davies, who writes:

'The laws which enable the universe to come into being spontaneously seem themselves to be the product of exceedingly ingenious design. If physics is the product of design, the universe must have a purpose, and the evidence of modern physics suggests strongly to me that the purpose includes us.'

An instructive (and entertaining) counterweight to this kind of metaphysical speculation is Bill Newton-Smith's essay 'The Origin of the Universe'.

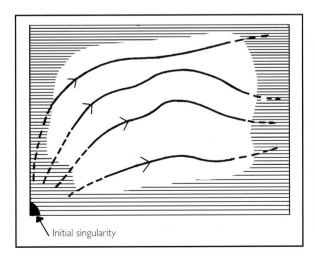

Initial singularity

In this diagram, the lines represent possible histories of the universe and the shaded area is 'quantum fuzz . . . where no notions of space and time exist'.

Well, the meaningfulness of words like 'initial' or 'singularity' (or of course 'event' or 'cause') may reasonably be doubted if the notions of time and space are disallowed. Doesn't 'initial' mean 'first', and doesn't 'first' presuppose a sequence in time? If, for example, the singularity is supposed to arise from the ferment of virtual particles in the preceding emptiness, notions of time, and perhaps space too, seem to have crept back in.

Be that as it may. Halliwell's 'initial singularity' is at any rate a beginning of sorts, and the question now is whether we do better to regard it as an unknowable mystery shrouded in 'quantum fuzz', or (following Plato, Aristotle and many others) as an analogue of a human thought. Sir James Jeans, for example, lined up with the teleologists when he said that the universe seems 'more like a great thought than a great machine'. It's true that this view posits what might look like an unnecessary entity – the great thought – in contravention of Ockham's razor. But if the alternative posits an 'event' or 'singularity' which is not just difficult to observe in practice, but completely unobservable in principle, is that better?

Perhaps the 'great thought' seems unscientific – if it does – because it goes against the flow. The evolution of our concept of causality (from purposes to impulses to correlations) shows a clear trend away from intuitively satisfying explanation and towards (mere) prediction. If saying that A causes B *only* means that A and B are correlated, then our wish to explain the correlation in terms of purposes or an intervening mechanism is an atavism, a kind of primitive urge which obstructs real science. On the other hand, our sense of an intuitively satisfying explanation is obviously still essential to present-day science, not only as a guide in theory-construction, but as a rationale for science itself.

Conclusion

Notice in conclusion that the arguments of this chapter do not *prove* that God exists. The most that can be said is that they suggest something like it. They would not justify any religious faith exceeding a modest hope that *something like* a protective human intelligence created the universe. This 'something' could as easily be a Platonic Craftsman struggling against recalcitrant material, as an omnipotent creator. It could, as Hume pointed out, be all sorts of things. But then, lots of other arguments don't prove what we would like them to. The argument from analogy (for the existence of other minds – Chapter 6) is in much worse shape, and according to Mill and others, it underpins our very strong conviction that other people think. I suppose enough has been said by now about the problems surrounding many of our fundamental beliefs. Anyone looking to score points off natural theology, then, as some still do, might be invited to get his own house in order first. And this is a consummation which is the more to be desired, because it's *our* house too.

In Hume's *Dialogues*, Philo has fun with some of the possibilities consistent with the argument from design:

'This world, for aught he knows, is very faulty and imperfect, compared to a superior standard; and was only the first rude essay of some infant deity, who afterwards abandoned it, ashamed of his lame performance: it is the work only of some dependent, inferior deity; and is the object of derision to his superiors: it is the product of old age and dotage in some superannuated deity; and ever since his death, has run on at adventures . . .'

Hume accepts the inference to *some* resemblance between a human maker and the first cause of the universe, but emphasises that a Christian wants rather more than that.

Do you agree . . . ?

1. **The human eye has obviously been designed for vision.**

   _____

2. **The suitability of earth for human life cannot be a mere coincidence.**

   _____

3. **There must be a first cause.**

   _____

4. **Our grounds are about equally strong for believing that God, and that other minds, exist.**

   _____

CHAPTER 26

Philosophy

In this final chapter, we turn the critical skills and insights we have been using, back on themselves. Do they have any shared distinguishing features? Can we rely on them to lead to truth?

Now that you've seen something (to be frank, a *little*) of philosophy, we can end with another question philosophers disagree about. As usual, we have a number of answers to the question, each of which seems reasonable to some philosophers some of the time, but none of which commands universal assent. The question is simply: what is philosophy?

Philosophy, according to the word's Greek origins, ought to be the love of wisdom. Etymology, however, is not much help to us here. What are we to understand by 'wisdom'?

Philosophy doesn't seem to be a science (science being rooted etymologically in 'knowledge'). It doesn't essentially involve experiment or field work and it doesn't yield predictions. Yet neither does it seem to turn on matters of taste and interpretation (like literary criticism), or on matters of fact and interpretation (like history), or on matters of right and interpretation (like law). Think back over the issues we've been looking at. What *kind* of issues have they been?

In this chapter, I'm going to throw all pretence of objectivity to the wind and tell you what *I* think philosophy is. Bear in mind that lots of philosophers much more famous than I am, would disagree.

The network of concepts

We can begin with the fact that some of our concepts are more important to us, more deeply embedded in our way of life, than others. We could probably manage without a concept of alimony or the deflationary spiral or perspective in art. A recognisably human life is possible without these relatively dispensable concepts. But it's hard to see, on the other hand, how we could manage without a concept of causality, or knowledge, or freedom.

Now the more deeply-embedded a concept is, the more widely its influence is felt, both in our lives and in its relations with other concepts. A deep concept has implications for many of the higher-level concepts, implications which may sometimes be straightforward, but which may also be

SCIENCE	{ how does science progress? how does induction work?
MIND	{ do ideas really exist? do mind and body causally interact? do other people have minds?
FREEDOM	{ is freedom just absence of constraint? is morality just enlightened self-interest?
KNOWLEDGE	{ how should we define knowledge? is anything *certain*? do our ideas resemble external things? is there a self?
LANGUAGE	{ are meanings ideas? how do we name, classify, communicate?
OBJECTIVITY	{ what is truth? is reality independent of us?
GOD	{ does God necessarily exist? is the first cause like a thought?

fugitive and subtle. It follows, if we want to understand our network of concepts, that working out these implications, seeing them clearly, is a matter of some importance. This struggle towards a perspicuous overview of conceptual relationships is one motivation for doing philosophy.

A more immediate motivation arises from conceptual conflict. As with any human structure built up over a long period, we naturally find changes of intention, shifts of style and substance, fracture-lines in the fabric of our conceptual scheme. A mid-level concept, such as the concept of a moral right, or the concept of probability, or the concept of introspection, may be in tension with one or another of the deep concepts. Or by way of one or another of the deep concepts, it may be incompatible with some other mid-level concept. In any of these various cases of conflict, alternative routes out of the problem, with *their* implications, have to be mapped out.

In addition to the definite conflicts we inherit, our concepts are subject to ongoing pressures to change. Philosophers must certainly know something about the external pressures affecting the concepts they are most interested in – such as the scientific pressures on the concept of a cause – but their particular, professional concern is with concept-to-concept influences. When someone has an interesting new idea – like computer processing, votes for women, cloning, rights for animals – it elbows its way into the existing network of concepts. Philosophers try to get clear about the relations between these existing concepts and their bold new neighbour.

Unfortunately, the relations between concepts are bewilderingly numerous, and any two concepts will almost certainly be connectable by many routes at once. How can we identify the most important connections? The central methods of philosophy – the Socratic search for definitions, the post-Cartesian search for defences against doubt, transcendentalism, the contemporary search for truth conditions or assertibility conditions – all these can best be understood as strategies for keeping to the most important pathways in the maze. Imperfect strategies, of course. Peter Strawson (1919–) says, '. . . philosophy, which takes human thought in general as its field . . . is so complex and many-sided . . . that any individual philosopher's work . . . must at best emphasise some aspects of the truth, to the neglect of others.' Iris Murdoch once said that philosophy is too difficult for human beings, and this is not a view one can dismiss out of hand.

The purpose of philosophy

So again, why do we do it? It would be nice to have a coherent, well-understood set of concepts of course, but perhaps that's not as essential as logicians are inclined to think. Perhaps we can muddle through with

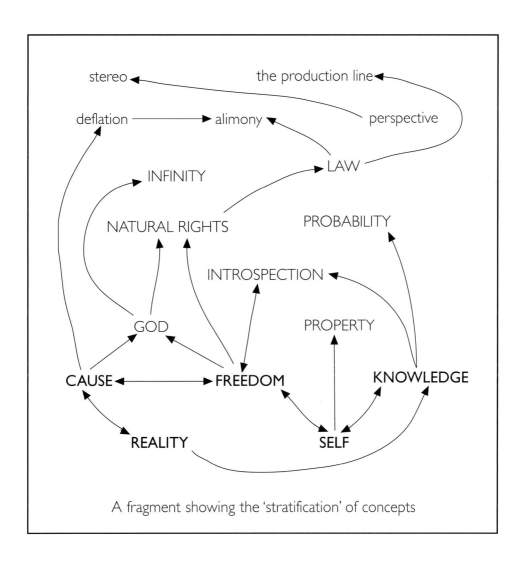

A fragment showing the 'stratification' of concepts

John Stuart Mill on philosophy:

'... philosophy, which to the superficial appears a thing so remote from the business of life and the outward interests of men, is in reality the thing on earth which most influences them, and in the long run overbears every other influence save those which it must itself obey.' *Essay on Bentham* (1838)

conflicting concepts, as long as they don't conflict too often or too publicly (the wave/particle duality of contemporary physics is a case in point). Another motivation is that conceptual evolution is interesting in itself. If the evolution of the fig wasp deserves study (and it does), so does the evolution of our conceptual system.

But perhaps the fundamental motivations are selfish, or at least, self-regarding. First, our concepts *of ourselves* are in the mix. They too are changing under all kinds of external pressures, and with all kinds of internal realignments of stress. It is no accident that all the concepts we have been looking at bear very intimately on who and what we are. If the core notion of a cause is purpose, then there is a purpose for *us*. If the core notion is mechanistic, we are machines. And so on. Secondly, the network of our concepts is what we think with: it *defines* us, at a given point in history, as creatures who can think. It follows that a change in any of our deep concepts is a change in who and what we are.

Philosophers (say I) are the attendants of this kind of change. Their business is to monitor the stresses set up by external and internal pressures on our concepts, as far as humanly possible, and to find ways in which our conceptual system might grow in response to them. If mathematics deals with the logical relations between numbers (relations which are in some areas stable and in other areas evolving) then philosophy, we can say, is concept-mathematics. Like mathematics, it does not involve experiment or field work, but deals with 'eternal' truths. And again like mathematics, although it *can* have fairly immediate practical effects, over a decade or two perhaps, its real importance is more general, on a time-scale of centuries. On the other hand, philosophy is unlike mathematics in that it can rarely hope for the compulsion of a proof. Compared with numbers, concepts are too rich and ill-defined.

Concept-mathematics

If we accept this idea of philosophy as concept-mathematics, one happy consequence is that philosophers' endemic disagreements become not only something to be expected, but something positively good. When philosophers disagree, they are in fact exploring different ways in which concepts might evolve, different routes out of some conceptual predicament. The same idea explains the tendency of philosophy to raise questions which, as Socrates said, paralyse us like a sting-ray. Philosophy appears to create or delight in questions with no answer (as you've probably discovered in the 'Do you agree?' sections) because its questions spring from areas of conceptual inadequacy or conflict. A philosophical problem is a place where we do not (yet) have the concepts to see how the problem might be solved. This means

Richard Rorty (1931–) on the nature of philosophy:

'Interesting philosophy is rarely an examination of the pros and cons of a thesis. Usually it is, implicitly or explicitly, a contest between an entrenched vocabulary which has become a nuisance and a half-formed new vocabulary which vaguely promises great things.'
Contingency, Irony and Solidarity (1989)

According to Rorty, philosophy does not discover, or assist in the discovery of, anything true of an independent world. Rejecting a tradition which stretches at least from Locke to Quine, he thinks of himself 'as auxiliary to the poet rather than to the physicist', but regards that as no demotion, since:

'. . . scientists invent descriptions of the world which are useful for the purposes of predicting and controlling what happens, just as poets and political thinkers invent other descriptions of it for other purposes. But there is no sense in which *any* of these descriptions is an accurate representation of the way the world is in itself.'

Rorty's radical pragmatism has (it seems to me) two main sources of strength. I think we must concede,
1. that we cannot give a paper explanation of what correspondence between a representation of the world and the world itself might be (see Chapter 22),
2. that philosophy (like science and poetry and any other human activity) is conditioned by cultural, linguistic and psychological factors. Philosophy is 'its time grasped in thought' – a point Rorty credits to Hegel.
However, neither of these points, as far as I can see, requires us to give up the concept of an independent world which we can represent more or less accurately, and know more or less directly.

that the business of philosophy is to think the currently unthinkable. No wonder it seems hard.

Mathematics divides into pure and applied, and in the same way, we can distinguish between pure philosophy, the cerebral business of working out the relations between concepts in the abstract, and the flesh and blood business of applying these conceptual relations to the world and our way of living in it. This little book has concentrated on the cerebral side because I think I see a pattern in it – the development, and in the seventeeth century, rejection, of the concept of natural purpose. But let me say explicitly that, as in mathematics, the application of the abstract stuff to concrete realities is not only an important test of success for the pure philosopher, it also constitutes, like precedent in law, a working definition of what the pure philosopher really means.

The comparison with maths, finally, also makes the relations between philosophy and science clear. It's possible to do concept-mathematics with any interesting concept, and there are of course interesting concepts in science, as there are in politics or religion, literature or common sense. Some concepts involve more technical knowledge than others. Religious concepts like prayer or transubstantiation, for example, or literary concepts like fiction or metaphor, or scientific concepts like evidence or complementarity might involve so much induction into the field, that a non-practitioner should go carefully indeed. At the same time, a non-practitioner's perspective can be important, if he or she brings an awareness of parallel situations involving other concepts, an awareness of the interconnectedness of concepts, an awareness of methods and strategies used elsewhere in concept-mathematics. There is no need to see philosophy as either underlabourer to the sciences or master of them, no need to identify it as a literary rather than scientific discipline. Concept evolution happens everywhere.

Conclusion

The whole enterprise of our culture – our Tower of Babel – heaves itself towards the sky, towards its imagined meeting-place with God. Always building – shedding great slabs of masonry and replacing them with others. Around it and inside it, philosophers do the things they do, mostly without effect, or finding only oblivion in some briefly terrifying fall. Competing voices. The dust and racket of making and destroying. And yet somehow, now and then, an Aristotle, or Descartes, or Hume makes an enduring difference.

And since that is a difference in who and what we are, it seems that philosophy is as important (for us) as it is difficult. One of those polarising facts, like the brevity of life, with an equal propensity to discourage and inspire.

Look – no foundations

In the best versions of the Indian rope trick, when the wise man has climbed to the top of the rope, he pulls it up after him and remains, unsupported, in mid-air. Well, the thread we have climbed up has been the history of changes in the concept of a cause: I have presented most of the central problems of modern philosophy as if they were created by those changes. Time now to pull this thread up after us by saying that the concept of a cause itself changed as a result of numerous historical and philosophical developments – Luther's concept of divine justice as much as geographical discovery, the rediscovery of Greek scepticism as much as better telescopes and guns. We used the causal theme only as an illustration of the interconnectedness of philosophical problems, not as an unmoved mover in the history of ideas.

Here's another disappearing trick. We have made considerable use of the idea that to be real is to have a causal role. Had you noticed that this is circular? Only a *real* causal role (as opposed to an imagined or legendary one) would establish the thing's reality. So we do not after all have a test of reality. I leave it to the conscientious reader to start at page 1, and go through the book again, making the necessary adjustments.

Do you agree . . . ?

1. **Philosophers have only interpreted the world: what matters is to change it.**

    _____

2. **There will be no end to the troubles of states, or indeed of humanity itself, until philosophers become kings in this world.**

    _____

3. **Philosophy simply puts everything before us, and neither explains nor deduces anything.**

    _____

4. **Philosophy is to science as the roots of a tree are to the trunk.**

    _____

Postscript

It would be a pity to end this 'overview' of the subject's history without saying something rash about its future. So here's a prediction. If it does not come true in my lifetime, I shall not be too surprised.

I said at the end of the last chapter that changes in the concept of a cause were themselves the result of other changes. But even if changes in the concept of a cause are not to be seen as a prime mover in the history of ideas, still, they do seem to correlate rather nicely with philosophy's golden ages.

Plato and Aristotle emerged from a struggle between teleologists and atomists. Anaxagoras and Diogenes of Apollonia in physics, Empedocles in biology, Socrates in ethics and psychology – all agreed on the importance of purpose, against the atomistic view of Leucippus and Democritus, later endorsed by Epicurus and Lucretius, that everything could be explained by random movements of atoms. Atomism, at that point, was an idea whose time had not yet come, and the triumph of teleology was confirmed in Plato, for whom there is a grand, overarching purpose for the universe, provided by an external artificer, or alternatively in Aristotle, who holds that things naturally tend towards a final state of their own.

Philosophy's second golden age – the age of Descartes and Hobbes, Hume and Kant – occurred because Aristotle's concept of a final cause had failed, and the idea of an external providence, though still immensely important to Copernicus and Kepler, Descartes and Newton, did not help to sharpen or give content to scientific investigation. People suddenly came to believe that they could do science without teleology. Whatever else it did, this piece of conceptual evolution certainly made work for philosophers to do.

It now seems, however, that the pendulum has swung too far. We live with the growing realisation that *some* concept of purpose or tendency-towards-an-end is indispensable. Philosophy's next golden age will dawn (to come to my prediction at last) when somebody has a really good idea about what sort of concept this ought to be. The main problems which will lie in this enterprising person's way are to provide some general guidance about:

1. when and how we are justified in reading a tendency-towards-an-end into a sequence of brute events,
2. when and how we are justified in distinguishing self-originated tendencies from externally imposed ones,
3. the implications of this new concept for causality, reality, freedom, knowledge and the rest.

   I wish him, or her, the very best of luck.

Causality and politics

The causal lens we have been using throughout this book has brought two points into focus:

1. that much of the agenda of modern philosophy has been set by the seventeenth-century rejection of teleological explanation, and
2. that the theory of causality we adopt has far-reaching consequences for the things we can say about other problems in philosophy – illustrating the general interconnectedness of philosophical problems.

Here's a final example to consolidate both points. Political philosophy is principally concerned with the question of obedience to government. Why should people do what governments tell them? Under what circumstances should they disobey, or revolt?

These questions suddenly became pressing in the seventeeth century, partly because of the wars of religion which followed the Reformation. But perhaps the political theories of Bodin, Hooker, Grotius, Filmer, Hobbes and Locke also owe something to the rejection of teleology.

What connection might there be between Aristotelian final causes and the justification of government authority? On the final causes way of thinking, things have an end state to which they naturally tend. Fire naturally tends to rise to the stars; stones naturally tend to rejoin the earth; plants and animals naturally tend towards a state in which they can reproduce.

People too have a natural end state, which in the most general terms (according to Aristotle) is to live rationally in a city-state. But seen in more detail, people do of course differ from each other, and for some, the natural end state is to rule. Others are simply born to serve. In this way, Aristotle found it easy to accept the institution of slavery. And the same kind of thinking makes a stratified feudal society seem entirely natural: it is as natural for the king to rule and the serf to toil as it is for fire to rise and a stone to fall.

Disallow the idea of a natural end state or final cause, and the power structure which has evolved in a given society suddenly seems, no longer pre-ordained, but 'just the way things happen to be now'. Explaining why things *ought* to be this way, or some other way, suddenly becomes – quite literally – a matter of life and death.

Bibliography

(listing works mentioned, many of which are available in several editions)

Anselm, *Proslogion*. B. Davies and G. R. Evans (eds), Oxford University Press, 1998.

Aristotle, *De Interpretatione*.

—, *Metaphysics*. Both in, for example, R. McKeon and R. P. McKeon (eds), Random House, 1941.

Arnauld, Antoine, *On True and False Ideas*. Edwin Mellen Press, 1990.

Bacon, Francis, *Novum Organum*. M. Silverthorne and L. Jardine (eds), Cambridge University Press, 2000.

Bentham, Jeremy, *Introduction to the Principles of Morals and Legislation*. J. H. Burns, H. L. A. Hart and F. Rosen (eds), Clarendon Press, 1996.

Berkeley, George, *Principles of Human Knowledge*. R. Woolhouse (ed.), Penguin, 1988.

Berlin, Isaiah, *Four Essays on Liberty*. Oxford University Press, 1990.

Boethius, *The Consolations of Philosophy*. R. Green (trans.), Bobbs-Merrill, 1962.

Bradley, F. H., *Ethical Studies*. Oxford University Press, 1988.

Darwin, Charles, *The Origin of Species by Means of Natural Selection*. Modern Library, 1998.

Descartes, Rene, *Discourse on Method*.

—, *Principles of Philosophy*.

—, *Meditations*.

—, *Second Set of Replies*.

—, *Optics*. All in, for example, *Descartes: Selected Philosophical Writings*. J. Cottingham, R. Stoothoff and D. Murdoch (eds), Cambridge University Press, 1988.

Dummett, M., *Truth and Other Enigmas*. Harvard University Press, 1981.

Einstein, Albert, *Autobiographical Notes*. P. A. Schilpp (trans.), Open Court, 1991.

—, *The World As I See It*. Citadel Press, 1993.

Galileo, Galilei, *The Assayer* in *Discoveries and Opinions of Galileo*. S. Drake (ed.), Anchor, 1990.

Gassendi, Pierre de, *Paradoxes Against the Aristotelians* in *Selected Works of Pierre Gassendi*. C. B. Bush (trans./ed.), Johnson, 1972.

Helmholtz, Hermann, *Popular Lectures on Scientific Subjects*. E. Atkinson (trans.), Longmans, Green and Company, 1893.

Hobbes, Thomas, *De Corpore*. W. Molesworth (ed.), Bohm, 1839.

—, *Leviathan*. J. C. A. Gaskin (ed.), Oxford University Press, 1998.

Hogg, James, *The Private Memoirs and Confessions of a Justified Sinner*. Knopf, 1992.

Hume, David, *Treatise of Human Nature*. See, for example, E. C. Mossner (ed.), Viking Press, 1986.

—, *Enquiry Concerning Human Understanding*. P. H. Nidditch (ed.), Clarendon Press, 1975.

—, *Dialogues Concerning Natural Religion*.

—, *Natural History of Religion*. Both in *Principal Writings on Religion*. J. C. A. Gaskin (ed.), Oxford University Press, 1998.

Huxley, T. H., *Hume*. Macmillan, 1879.

James, William, *Pragmatism*. See, for example, B. Kuklick (ed.), Library of America, 1988.

Jourdain, R., *Music, the Brain & Ecstasy*. Avon Books, 1998.

Kant, Immanuel, *Prolegomena to Any Future Metaphysics*. G. Hatfield (ed.), Cambridge University Press, 1997.

—, *Critique of Pure Reason*. See, for example, P. Guyer and A. W. Wood (eds), Cambridge University Press, 1999.

—, *Fundamental Principles of the Metaphysic of Morals*. T. K. Abbott (ed.), Prentice Hall, 1949.

Laplace, Pierre, *A Philosophical Essay on Probabilities*. Dover, 1996.

Leibniz, Gottfried, *Monadology*. G. R. Montgomery (trans.), Prometheus, 1992.

Locke, John, *An Essay Concerning Human Understanding*. Prometheus, 1994.

Mill, John Stuart, *An Examination of Sir William Hamilton's Philosophy*. University of Toronto Press, 1979.

—, *Utilitarianism*.

—, 'Essay on Bentham'. Both in *Utilitarianism and Other Essays*. A. Ryan (ed.), Viking, 1987.

Malebranche, Nicolas, *Search After Truth*. T. M. Lennon and P. J. Olscamp (eds), Cambridge University Press, 1997.

Marx, Karl, *Towards a Critique of Hegel's Philosophy of Right* in *The Marx-Engels Reader*. R. C. Tucker (ed.), W. W. Norton, 1978.

Nagel, T., 'What is it Like to be a Bat?' reprinted in, for example, *Modern Philosophy of Mind*. W. Lyons (ed.), Everyman, 1995.

Newton-Smith, W., 'The Origin of the Universe', reprinted in *Time in Contemporary Intellectual Thought*. P. J. N. Baert (ed.), Elsevier Science, 2000.

Place, U. T., 'Is Consciousness a Brain Process?', reprinted in, for example, *Modern Philosophy of Mind*. W. Lyons (ed.), Everyman, 1995.

Plato, *Sophist*. E. Brann (trans.), Focus, 1996.

—, *Republic*. See, for example, D. Lee (trans.), Viking, 1979.

—, *Phaedo*. See, for example, *The Last Days of Socrates*. H. Tredennick and H. Tarrant (eds), Penguin, 1995.

Popper, Karl, *Conjectures and Refutations*. Routledge, 1992.

Priestley, J., *Letters to a Philosophical Unbeliever*. Johnson, 1787, vol. 1.

Putnam, H., 'Philosophy and our Mental Life', reprinted in, for example, *Modern Philosophy of Mind*. W. Lyons (ed.), Everyman, 1995.

Quine, W. V., 'The Problem of Meaning in Linguistics' in *From a Logical Point of View*. Harvard University Press, 1980.

—, *Word and Object*. MIT Press, 1964.

Ramsay, F., 'Facts and Propositions' in *Philosophical Papers*. H. Mellor (ed.), Cambridge University Press, 1990.

Reid, Thomas, *An Inquiry into the Human Mind*. D. R. Brookes (ed.), Edinburgh University Press, 2000.

Ridley, B. K., *Time, Space and Things*. Cambridge University Press, 1995.

Rorty, R., *Consequences of Pragmatism*. University of Minnesota Press, 1985.

—, *Contingency, Irony, and Solidarity*. Cambridge University Press, 1989.

Russell, Bertrand, *History of Western Philosophy*. Allen and Unwin, 1921.

—, *The Analysis of Mind*. Allen and Unwin, 1921.

Ryle, Gilbert, *The Concept of Mind*. University of Chicago Press, 1984.

Saussure, Ferdinand de, *Course in General Linguistics*. McGraw-Hill, 1965.

Schopenhauer, Arthur, *The World as Will and Representation*. Everyman, 1919.

Searle, John, *Intentionality*. Cambridge University Press, 1983.

Skinner, B. F., *Science and Human Behaviour*. Free Press, 1965.

Spinoza, Benedict de, *Ethics*. G. H. R. Parkinson (ed.), Oxford University Press, 2000.

Tomasello, Michael, *The Cultural Origins of Human Cognition*. Harvard University Press, 2001.

Waugh, Evelyn, *The Ordeal of Gilbert Pinfold*. Chapman and Hall, 1957.

Wittgenstein, Ludwig, *Philosophical Investigations*. G. E. M. Anscombe (trans.), Prentice Hall, 1999.

—, *On Certainty*. G. E. M. Anscombe and G. H. von Wright (eds), HarperCollins, 1986.

Acknowledgements

Grateful acknowledgement is made to the following copyright holders for permission to reproduce material in this book. Every effort has been made to trace copyright holders but if any have inadvertently been overlooked, the publishers will be pleased to make the necessary arrangements at the first opportunity.

AKG London for Karl Popper (1981); Dimitri Ivanovich Mendelev (colour drawing after a photograph taken in 1900); Thomas Hobbes; Aristotle (photo by Erich Lessing); Galileo (drawing by Ottavio Leoni); Nicolas Malebranche (crayon engraving, 1762, by Jean Charles Francois after a drawing by Bachelier); Immanuel Kant; William James (Pach, New York, c. 1890); Ludwig Wittgenstein (photo by Moritz Naehr, Vienna, 1930); The Reid Project, Philosophy Department, University of Aberdeen for the Thomas Reid line drawing; The Whitworth Art Gallery, the University of Manchester for William Blake: 'Europe' Plate i: Frontispiece, *The Ancient of Days*; The Peirce Edition Project, Indiana University, Indianapolis, Indiana for the photograph of Charles S. Peirce; The Scottish National Portrait Gallery for David Hume by Allan Ramsay: In a private Scottish Collection; The National Galleries of Scotland for David Hume by Allan Ramsay; Hulton Getty for Alexander Fleming, c. 1950; BFI Stills, Posters and Designs for supplying the stills from *Modern Times* and *Compulsion*; Darryl F. Zanuck Productions, Inc. for the still from *Compulsion*; The V&A Picture library for the Chippendale Chair, mahogany, c. 1755; The Mary Evans Picture Library for René Descartes; Johannes Kepler; Nikolas Copernicus; John Locke; Antoine Arnauld (engraving by Delpech); George Berkeley and Saint Anselm; Popperfoto for Clarence Darrow; Bettmann/CORBIS for Francis Bacon; Archivo Iconografico, S. A./CORBIS for René Descartes by Sebastien Bourdon; E. O. Hoppé/CORBIS for the Chicago Street Scene; Hulton-Deutsch Collection/CORBIS for Mrs Egeland launching the liner *M. V. Bloemfontein Castle*; Powerstock Zefa for the new born baby crying; St.Mary's Hospital Medical School/Science Photo Library for the photograph of the original culture plate of the fungus *Penicillium notatum*; Shakespeare Centre Library, Stratford-upon-Avon for the photograph of Derek Jacobi in the Royal Shakespeare Company's 1993 production of *Macbeth*, photograph: Malcolm Davies.

Index

Note: Page references *in italics* refer to illustrations.

duty, 73

Einstein, Albert, 20, 100, 101, 201
Elisabeth, Princess of Bohemia, 38
empiricism, 41, 43, 88, 97, 98, 104, 105
eternity, 55
Evans, Gareth, 139
evolution, 196–8
    of concepts, 206–8
    of the eye, 199
existence, 122, 188–95; *see also* reality
existentialism, 70–2
experience, 102–3
    contents, 150–2
    and induction, 14–16
    reality of, 160–2
explanation, 144–8
    macro- or micro-, 146–8
    see also theory and data

fatalism, 54–60
Feynman, Richard, 156
fiction, 28
Fleming, Alexander, 4–8, *7*
freedom, 56–61, 64, 205
    meaning, 56–8
    negative, 57, 66
    positive, 57, 58, 66
functionalism, 162–4, 168
    in biology, 165

Galileo, Galilei, 3, 46, 82, *83*, 153
games, rules, 67
Gassendi, Pierre, 47, 88
generalisation, 176, 178
God, 38, 77, 181, *185*, 205
    Berkeley on, 92, 93, 184
    existence, 84, 188–95, 202
    idea of, 36
    need for, 184–6
    omniscience, 54, 184
gravity, 2, 3, 10, 38, 198

Grice, Paul, 148
Guanilo, 195

Halliwell, Jonathan, 200
happiness, 70, 71
Helmholtz, Hermann von, 157
Helmont, Jean Baptiste van, 46
Hobbes, Thomas, 46, *65*
    on classification, 120
    empiricism, 13
    on freedom, 56, 57
    on self-interest, 65
Hogg, James
    The Confessions of a Justified Sinner, 54
Hoyle, Fred, 201
Hull, Clark, 63
human nature, 68, 70–2
humanism, 78
Hume, David, 4, 11, *13*, 15, 18, 24, 66, 95, *99*, 102
    on beliefs, 116–18
    on causality, 10–12, 13, 34, 46, 64, 108, 110
    on ideas, 104, 106, 130
    on induction, 15, 16
    on miracles, 98–100, 101
    on necessary existence, 192, 193
    on reason, 62
    on resemblance, 130–2
    scepticism, 92, 94–100
    on the self, 96–8
    Dialogues Concerning Natural Religion, 196, 197, 200, 203
    Natural History of Religion, 197
    Treatise of Human Nature, 10–14, 15, 94–8, 113, 117, 131
Hutcheson, Francis, 71
Huxley, T. H., 37

idealism, 90, 92
    transcendental, 119
ideas, 159
    a priori, 104